CONTENTS

Cover photo: USS *Yorktown* (CV-10) anchored in harbor. (U.S. Naval Institute photo archive)

Library of Congress Cataloging-in-Publication Data is available.

ISBN: 978-1-68247-981-0 (print)

ISBN: 978-1-68247-984-1 (eBook)

INTRODUCTION

Following World War I the aircraft carrier evolved as a new type of warship that during World War II would become the centerpiece of America's global naval power. The first American aircraft carrier, *Langley*, hull number CV-1, was a converted collier and served primarily as an experimental ship to develop techniques for carrier operations. The next two carriers, *Lexington* (CV-2) and *Saratoga* (CV-3), converted from unfinished battle cruisers, became the U.S. Navy's first really effective fleet carriers. *Ranger* (CV-4) was the first American carrier built from the keel up, but, her design constrained by the Washington Naval Treaty of 1922, she proved too slow to operate with the fast carrier forces in the Pacific during World War II.

Yorktown (CV-5) and *Enterprise* (CV-6), laid down in 1934 and commissioned in 1937 and 1938, were a highly successful design that applied the lessons learned with previous ships. They proved large enough to be useful in carrier operations, with a good blend of size, speed, and aircraft-carrying capacity. They formed the basis of what would become the *Essex* class. They were followed by *Wasp* (CV-7), which was similar in size to the *Ranger* but with features of the *Yorktown* class. The last carrier completed before the war was *Hornet* (CV-8), which was essentially an improved *Yorktown*.

All images are official U.S. Navy photos unless otherwise indicated.

This *Yorktown*, the U.S. Navy's fourth vessel of that name, would carry on in the tradition of her predecessor and ultimately be preserved as a museum ship. In 1974, the Navy approved the donation of *Yorktown* to the Patriot's Point Development Authority in Charleston, South Carolina. She was formally dedicated as a memorial on 13 October 1975, the two-hundredth anniversary of the Navy. This is her story.

Yorktown **(CV-5) anchored in Hampton Roads, Virginia, 30 October 1937. (NHHC/NH)**

Yorktown's Predecessors
A Gallant Heritage

The first *Yorktown* was a sloop named for the climactic battle of the American Revolution, fought in 1781. Laid down in the Norfolk Navy Yard, she was commissioned in 1840 and served in the Pacific, protecting American whaling ships and the nation's ocean trade. She returned to New York in 1843 and was decommissioned. Activated the following year, she joined the patrol off Africa to curtail the slave trade, capturing three slave ships. She was again decommissioned in Boston in 1846. In 1848 she was recommissioned yet again to patrol off the African coast, but in September 1850 she struck an uncharted reef in the Cape Verde Islands. Although she quickly broke up, no lives were lost in the wreck.

The second *Yorktown*, Gunboat Number 1, was a steel-hulled, twin-screw vessel laid down in the William Cramp & Sons shipyard in Philadelphia. Commissioned in 1889, she joined the "Squadron of Evolution" as it developed tactical maneuvers for the new steel-hulled naval vessels then coming into service. She also operated in European waters and the Mediterranean, making port calls in Portugal, Spain, Morocco, France, Italy, Greece, and Malta. In 1891 she was transferred to the Pacific Squadron and responded to violence in which American sailors were attacked that had broken out following a disputed election in Chile. After a month of showing the flag in Valparaiso she departed in January 1892 for Peru with refugees from the American, Spanish, and Italian legations. When tensions between Chile and the United States cooled, she steamed north for repairs at the Mare Island shipyard. That spring she headed toward Arctic waters, along with two other naval vessels and three revenue cutters, to protect herds of seals in the Bering Sea from poachers. In 1894 she sailed to the western

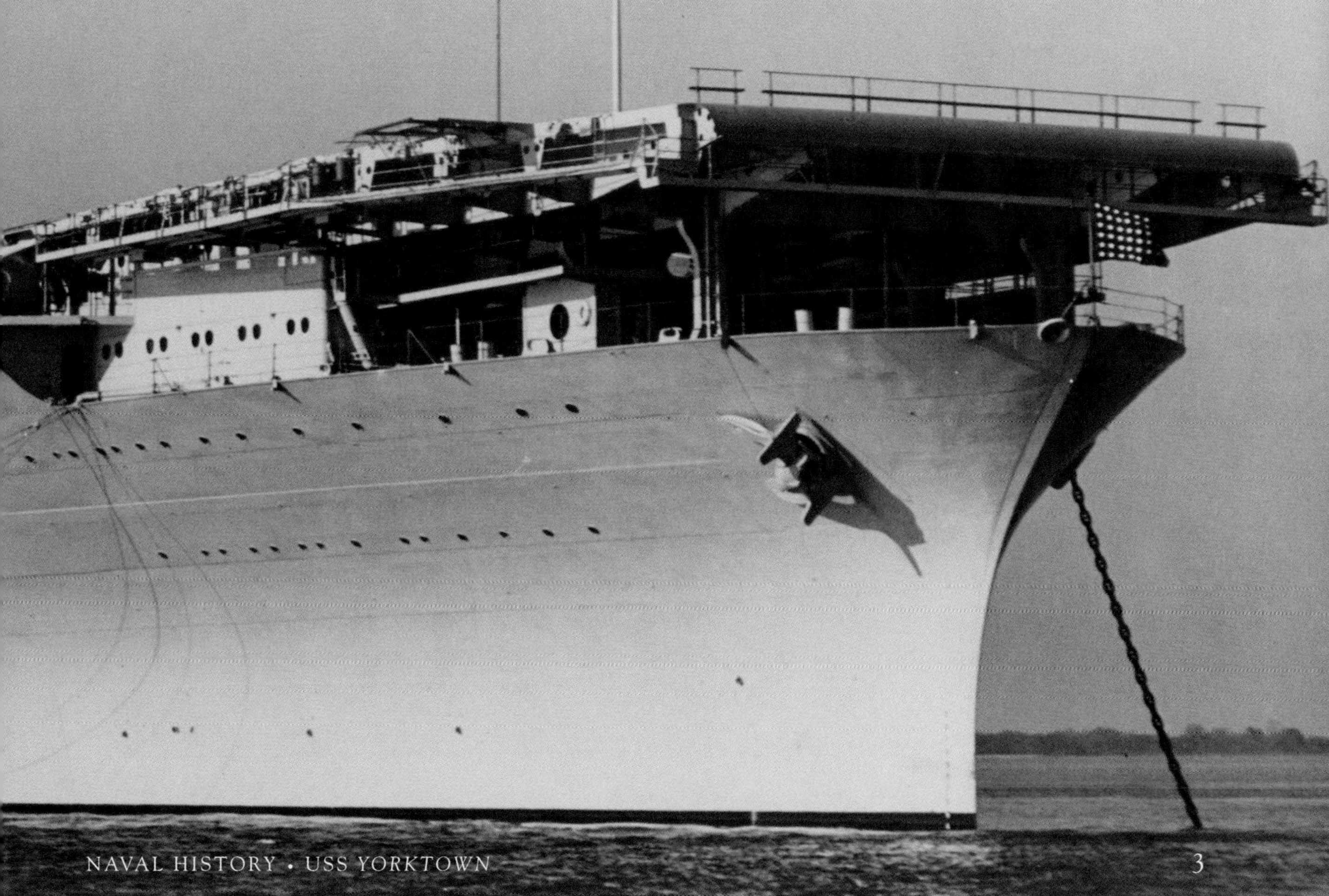

Pacific for duty on the Asiatic Station. Laid up and decommissioned at Mare Island in 1897, she was inactive during the Spanish-American War, which began in 1898. Recommissioned in November of that year, she headed for the Philippines to deal with violence instigated by "*insurrectos*," Filipino guerillas. In 1900, during the Boxer Rebellion, she operated off the coast of northern China before returning to the Philippines to support Army pacification efforts. Back at Mare Island in 1903, she was decommissioned but was recommissioned in 1906 to protect American interests off the west coasts of Mexico, Honduras, and Nicaragua. Decommissioned at Mare Island for alterations in 1912, she was recommissioned the following year and resumed her duties protecting American interests off the west coast of Latin America. With America's entry in World War I she operated off the East Coast escorting coastal convoys. Returning to Mare Island in 1919 she was placed out of commission and sold in 1921.

The third *Yorktown*, hull number CV-5, was the lead ship of a new class of aircraft carriers. She was laid down on 21 May 1934 at the Newport News Shipbuilding and Dry Dock Company in Newport News, Virginia. She was launched on 4 April 1936, sponsored by the first lady, Eleanor Roosevelt, and was commissioned at the Norfolk Naval Base on 30 September 1937 with Capt. Ernest D. McWhorter in command. She operated in both the Atlantic and Pacific, participating in various fleet exercises. When the Japanese attacked Pearl Harbor on 7 December 1941 *Yorktown* was in port at Norfolk after service in the Neutrality Patrol. *Ranger, Wasp*, and the newly commissioned *Hornet* remained in the Atlantic, but *Yorktown* departed for the Pacific to join *Enterprise*, *Lexington*, and *Saratoga*. Her first mission was to escort a convoy carrying Marine reinforcements to American Samoa. Later, while Task Force 8, built around *Enterprise*, headed for strikes against the Marshall Islands, Task Force 17 with *Yorktown* set out on what would be the first American offensive of the war, in the Gilberts. At the beginning of February 1942 *Yorktown*'s air group delivered strikes on Jaluit, Makin, and Mili, but adverse weather limited their effectiveness, and further strikes were canceled. *Yorktown* returned to Pearl Harbor and replenished there before sailing for the Coral Sea.

On 6 March, she rendezvoused with a task force built around *Lexington* and headed toward Rabaul and Gasmata to attack Japanese shipping. However, when word was received of Japanese landings in the Huon Gulf on 7 March, the objective changed to Japanese shipping in the Lae–Salamaua area. On the morning of 10 March the American carriers launched strikes from the Gulf of Papua, the aircraft flying over the Owen Stanley Mountains and achieving complete surprise. The carriers then retired. *Yorktown* and *Lexington* were in the Coral Sea when the Japanese determined that their next objective would be Port Moresby on the southern coast of New Guinea. They landed on Tulagi in the Solomons to set up a seaplane base in support of that invasion. At daybreak on 4 May *Yorktown* launched a strike on the Japanese beachhead on Tulagi. Meanwhile, Japanese troop transports, escorted by destroyers and the light carrier *Shoho*, were heading for Port Moresby. They were protected by the fleet carriers

Shokaku and *Zuikaku*. The opposing carrier groups sought each other out on the 5th and 6th, and on the morning of 7 May Japanese carrier planes sank the American destroyer *Sims* and the oiler *Neosho* while American planes sank the *Shoho*. On 8 May Japanese aircraft sank *Lexington* and damaged *Yorktown*; on the Japanese side *Shokaku* was so damaged that she had to retire, and *Zuikaku* had lost so many planes that the Port Moresby invasion, now without adequate air cover, was deferred and ultimately canceled. The battle in the Coral Sea marked the first naval engagement in which neither side sighted the opposing force. Although tactically the Japanese had inflicted more damage, the Allies had won strategically in preventing the invasion of Port Moresby. *Yorktown* limped back to Pearl Harbor and through herculean efforts was able to return to sea in time to participate in the battle that would mark the turning point in the war in the Pacific—the battle of Midway, between 4 and 7 June.

The four Japanese carriers that took part, *Akagi*, *Kaga*, *Soryu*, and *Hiryu*, had been among the six that had attacked Pearl Harbor—Coral Sea had left *Shokaku* and *Zuikaku* unable to participate. The Japanese had assumed that the attack on Midway would catch the Americans by surprise and lure their remaining carriers into a trap. As it turned out American intelligence had predicted the attack, and the carriers *Enterprise* and *Hornet*, returned from the Doolittle Raid on Tokyo in April, along with the hastily repaired *Yorktown* with a scratch air group, were ready to ambush the Japanese. The four Japanese carriers, along with a cruiser, would be lost. *Enterprise* and *Hornet* would survive the battle. *Yorktown*'s Devastator torpedo bombers were savaged, but her Dauntless dive-bombers turned *Soryu* into a flaming wreck while *Enterprise* dive-bombers did the same for *Akagi* and *Kaga*. However, the fourth, *Hiryu*, was spared the initial onslaught and launched a strike that found *Yorktown*. The American carrier's Wildcat fighters put up a vigorous defense and her antiaircraft batteries took on the remaining torpedo planes and dive-bombers, but three dive-bombers scored hits.

Yorktown slowed to a stop. She was dead in the water for a time but managed to get under way again that afternoon and was preparing for flight operations when another raid came in. Her fighters took on this raid, and she maneuvered radically to avoid two torpedo attacks, but two torpedoes hit her port side. She lost power and again went dead in the water, with a jammed rudder and an increasing list to port. Fearing that she would soon capsize, Capt. Elliott Buckmaster ordered her abandoned. But the stubborn *Yorktown* remained afloat through the night and salvage efforts were under way by the next day. The destroyer *Hammann* was alongside to assist when a Japanese submarine slipped inside *Yorktown*'s protective screen and launched a spread of four torpedoes at her starboard side. One hit *Hammann*, which broke in two and sank quickly. Two torpedoes hit *Yorktown*, and the fourth passed astern. Salvage efforts were suspended, but the next morning, as she was still afloat, they resumed. But by this time her list had increased dramatically, and soon she rolled over and sank. It was a sad end to a gallant ship, but her legacy would be carried on by her namesake.

THE FIGHTING LADY

The story of *Yorktown* began when she was laid down as *Bon Homme Richard* (CV-10) at the Newport News Shipbuilding & Dry Dock Company in Newport News, Virginia, on 1 December 1941, only six days before the attack on Pearl Harbor. She was renamed *Yorktown* on 26 September 1942 and on 21 January 1943 was ready for launching. Eleanor Roosevelt was her sponsor, as she had been for her predecessor. Rear Adm. Elliott Buckmaster, who had been captain of the old *Yorktown*, was giving a speech praising the shipyard workers when, seven minutes early, *Yorktown* began to slide down the ways. The first lady gamely stepped up and grabbed the traditional bottle of champagne for the christening and swung it across the bow. It bounced off and she caught it, her second swing splattering the bottle

and showering her and Buckmaster with champagne.

Yorktown would aways be known afterward as an "eager" ship. Launch and christening only mark the beginning of the process of preparing a new warship for service; there is much work to be completed during the fitting-out process that follows.

The prospective captain of the new *Yorktown*, Capt. Joseph J. "Jocko" Clark, worked tirelessly with the shipyard and the new officers and crew reporting on board to complete the work ahead of schedule.

***Yorktown* sliding down the shipways into the James River moments after her christening. (NAVSOURCE)**

Just after noon on 15 April 1943 at Pier 4 in the Norfolk Navy Yard Rear Adm. Felix Gygax accepted *Yorktown* from her builders on behalf of the Navy. The Assistant Secretary of the Navy for Air, Artemus Gates, was present for the commissioning ceremony, as were several flag officers and Wesley E. Disney, a congressional representative from Oklahoma, Captain Clark's home state. The officers and crew were at quarters on the flight deck as the national anthem was played, the colors were flown, and the commissioning pennant was hoisted to the peak. Gates' flag was raised, the chaplain said an invocation, and *Yorktown* was placed in commission. Captain Clark read his orders, assumed command, and set the watch.

Gates then presented citations to several crew members for their service in the war heretofore. On completion of the ceremonies, the guests departed. *Yorktown* lit fires under her boilers and made her way to Dry Dock 4, where she was dry-docked for several days while inspections were completed and stores loaded. Finally, on the 27th, she prepared to get under way; when the dry-dock was flooded she made her way out to Chesapeake Bay, where she would ensure that she was seaworthy and that all equipment was in working order. Her new crew would also practice skills they would need later in combat. On 7 May Lt. Cdr. James H. "Jimmy" Flatley, commander of Air Group 5, flew the first plane—an F6F-3 Hellcat—on board.

(left) Eleanor Roosevelt christens *Yorktown* at her launch on 21 January 1943. The First Lady had christened the first *Yorktown* seven years before. Rear Adm. Elliot Buckmaster, last skipper of the previous *Yorktown*, is standing just behind Mrs. Roosevelt. (NAVSOURCE)

As a fighter pilot, Flatley had been on board the previous *Yorktown* for the Coral Sea battle. He had then returned to the United States to form Fighting Squadron 10 (VF-10), the "Grim Reapers," and commanded it on board *Enterprise* during the battle of the Santa Cruz Islands in October and the Naval Battle of Guadalcanal in November 1942.

He would be leading Air Group 5 into combat, but first he would have to mold it into a fighting team. At this point Air Group 5 was a "scratch" outfit composed of VF-1 (with F6F-3 Hellcats), Bombing Squadrons VB-4 and VB-6 (with SB2C-1 Helldivers), and VT-5 (with TBF-1 Avengers). The debut of the Helldivers during shakedown would prove a disaster; VB-4 and VB-6 would be reequipped with the SBD-5 Dauntless as a double squadron and redesignated VB-5 before entering combat.

Yorktown left the Chesapeake area on 21 May to begin her shakedown training near Trinidad. "Shakedown" is an apt Navy term for the difficult early operations of any new ship, but particularly so during wartime. The difficulties of learning the workings of a huge and complex physical plant were compounded by the need to transform a body of more than 2,500 officers and men, almost all of whom had never been to sea, into a cohesive crew. Many of the skills needed were taught at various schools and training centers ashore, but only constant drill and practice at sea could develop the teamwork needed to fight and win. Captains hold absolute responsibility for the combat readiness of their ships and for the safety, well-being, and efficiency of their crews. Their ability, experience, and leadership often determine what kind of personalities their ships develop.

Jocko Clark was born in the Cherokee Nation before it became part of Oklahoma and was commissioned from the U.S. Naval Academy as an ensign in 1917. He served in a variety of posts, including on board destroyers, before earning his "wings of gold" as a naval aviator in 1925. At the start of the war Clark was executive officer of the old *Yorktown* for the raids on the Gilbert and Marshall Islands. He later commanded the escort carrier *Suwannee* in the Atlantic, participating in the invasion of North Africa in November 1942, before being selected to command the new *Yorktown*. Proud of his Cherokee heritage, Clark was an aggressive leader who demanded the best from those under him. The

Yorktown's commissioning at the Norfolk Navy Yard on 15 April 1943. (U.S. Navy)

day before the *Yorktown*'s commissioning he advised his officers, "This ship will reach the combat zone in record time and in complete combat readiness. Therefore, any officer who remains on board will grade his own fitness report a perfect 4.0, since I will not tolerate anything less!" He was quick to criticize but just as quick to praise. If a method was unauthorized but produced the desired results, he would back it. His pilots knew that he would go to any length to rescue a pilot down at sea. He passed his experience in destroyers down to his officers of the deck so that *Yorktown* would always be smartly handled. *Yorktown* gained a reputation as a clean, happy, and squared-away ship, up to any challenge.

During her shakedown *Yorktown* hosted filmmakers. Arthur Radford, then a captain involved in naval air training, commissioned Edward Steichen, the

Lieutenant Commander Flatley on the first plane to land on *Yorktown*, 7 May 1943. (U.S. Navy)

famous photographer, to head up a unit to tell the story of the Navy's air war in the Pacific. Under Steichen were Lt. Dwight W. Long, who took motion pictures, and Lt. Charles W. Kerlee, who handled still photography. They would remain on board *Yorktown* through the Philippine Sea air battle; their footage would form the basis of the documentary *The Fighting Lady*, released in 1944. Cdr. Frank W. "Spig" Wead, an early naval aviator who had become a Hollywood screenwriter after a crippling accident, convinced his old friend Captain Clark to allow director Henry Hathaway to film background scenes on board for the movie *Wing and a Prayer*, a fictional account of the early Pacific air battles. Hathaway came on board in January 1944 to observe carrier operations and advise Dwight Long.

Returning to Norfolk on 17 June, *Yorktown* underwent a "limited availability" (i.e., during which her availability for operations would be limited, to some specific extent) for post-shakedown repairs. She completed repairs on 1 July and conducted air operations out of Norfolk until the 6th, when she departed for the Pacific. Transiting the Panama Canal on 11 July, she arrived at Pearl Harbor on 24 July and began a month of exercises in the Hawaiian Islands area. On 22 August 1943 she stood out from Pearl Harbor bound for her first combat operation of the war.

The Air Group

The basic unit of naval aviation is the squadron, its number of aircraft and crews varying with the type of aircraft and the current organizational doctrine. Early on, squadrons carried designations that reflected their missions. The *V* for heavier-than-air aircraft was followed by another letter—*F* for fighting, *B* for bombing, *S* for scouting, or *T* for torpedo—and the number of the squadron. Two or more squadrons assigned to a carrier formed the air group. Beginning in 1937, the term was associated with the name of the ship, for example, "*Saratoga* Air Group." When the air group commander became an authorized command billet the following year, the air group became a formal unit. (Previously all squadrons were under the command of the captain of the ship and the senior aviator in a given formation would be in tactical command.) At the start of the war a typical air group consisted of one fighting squadron with 18 Wildcats, one scouting and one bombing squadron each with 18 Dauntless dive-bombers, and one torpedo squadron with 18 Devastators.

In 1942 carrier air groups began to be numbered, and by the time *Yorktown* was commissioned a typical *Essex*-class carrier air group had a "double" fighting squadron of 36 F6F Hellcats, a bombing squadron with 36 SBD Dauntless dive-bombers, and a torpedo squadron with 18 TBF Avengers. Air Group 5 was on board *Yorktown* from August 1943 to May 1944; Air Group 1 relieved it that month while *Yorktown* was at Pearl Harbor and remained until August. After two months of overhaul at Bremerton, *Yorktown* embarked Air Group 3 in October 1944 when it redeployed to the western Pacific. As the war progressed, the need for more fighters led to an increase in the size of the fighting squadrons, while their bombing squadrons got smaller. The torpedo squadrons were equipped with the TBM, the version of the Avenger built by the Eastern Aircraft division of General Motors, and the SB2C Helldiver had replaced the Dauntless in Air Groups 1, 3, 9, and 88. Beginning in January 1944 carrier air groups began receiving specially equipped and trained night-fighter detachments flying modified Hellcats or Corsairs. By later in the war fighter squadrons had grown in size to the point where they were split in two, becoming fighter (VF) and fighter-bomber (VBF) squadrons, though in practice the two were interchangeable. When Air Group 9 deployed on board *Yorktown* in March 1945 it was organized in this manner. (Air Group 3 was also reorganized during its deployment.) The F4U Corsair, which had problems operating from carriers early in the war, began to equip carrier squadrons late in 1944 to help counter the growing kamikaze threat. The final change came in July 1945, as the war wound down, when Air Group 88's VBF squadron was reequipped with the FG-1, the version of the Corsair built by Goodyear.

Hellcat

F6F-3 Hellcats in the three-color camouflage pattern. (NNAM)

The Grumman F6F Hellcat succeeded the stubby little F4F Wildcat, the only Navy fighter that held its own against the superb Japanese Zero in the first year of Pacific combat. Looking like the Wildcat's younger but bigger brother, the Hellcat was unmistakably a product of the Grumman "Iron Works." It was chubby and angular but rugged, and it was powered by a magnificent engine, the 2,000-horsepower Pratt and Whitney R-2800 Double Wasp. With a wingspan of 42 feet 10 inches and a gross weight of nearly seven tons, the Hellcat was a lot of airplane but steady as a rock when coming on board a carrier. The Hellcat was the first Navy fighter designed on the basis of combat experience with the Zero, and it matched or exceeded the Zero's performance in nearly every category except low-speed maneuverability. The Hellcat's heavy armament of six .50-caliber machine guns could easily tear apart a Zero, and its self-sealing tanks, armor plate, and sturdy structure made it more survivable than its opposition.

Aircraft Colors and Markings

When Lieutenant Commander Flatley landed the first Hellcat on *Yorktown* it was painted in what had been the standard scheme of blue-gray with light-gray undersurfaces. The national insignia was a large blue disc with a white five-pointed star, and it appeared on the upper and lower surfaces of both wings. A large white 00 was painted ahead of the national insignia on the fuselage, marking the aircraft as belonging to the commander of the air group (CAG). During *Yorktown*'s shakedown the Hellcats, Helldivers, and Avengers of Air Group 5 were in painted in the nonspecular (nonreflective) three-color camouflage pattern of sea-blue upper surfaces, intermediate-blue sides, and insignia-white undersurfaces. (That, is, except for the Helldivers—the undersides of their outer wing panels, which folded upward, were painted intermediate blue.) Later the national insignia on the sides of the aircraft had white rectangles added, and they appeared only on the upper left and lower right wings. Its outline, originally red, was changed to blue, since red was associated with Japanese markings. In 1944 fighters began to be painted in overall glossy sea blue, which was applied to other carrier-based aircraft soon afterward (not all aircraft would be repainted during the war).

In 1944 individual air groups adopted "G symbols" that identified them, independently of particular carriers. For *Yorktown* this was a diagonal white stripe on the vertical tail. Green propeller spinners were also a *Yorktown* marking. In January 1945 a directive formalized the G symbols, which were now identified with specific carriers. *Yorktown* aircraft had a large white diagonal covering the trailing edge of the vertical tail. Also, a white triangle appeared on the upper-right wing tip.

The final change occurred in July 1945, when letters were specified instead of geometric designs, since they were more practical and simpler to describe over voice radio. The letters assigned to *Yorktown* were *RR*, on the vertical tail and the upper-right and lower-left wing tips. The letter system continued in use in the postwar period and evolved into the two-letter system still in use, in which the first letter is either A, denoting units assigned to the Atlantic Fleet, or *N* for the Pacific Fleet.

Dauntless

SBD-5 Dauntless dive-bombers, October 1943. (U.S. Navy)

The Douglas SBD Dauntless was the Navy's workhorse in the Pacific and the deciding factor in the battle of Midway, the turning point in the war against Japan. (It was the only aircraft to participate in all five engagements of the Pacific War fought exclusively between carriers.) This two-place dive-bomber was slow and vulnerable, but it possessed long range, good handling characteristics, maneuverability, a potent bombload, great diving characteristics, good defensive armament, and ruggedness and dependability that kept it in service long after its planned replacement by the Curtiss Helldiver. Considering its obsolescence even in the early part of the war, the Dauntless gave a good account of itself in tangles with Japanese fighters, its loss rate reportedly the lowest of any carrier aircraft. The SBD had a wingspan of 41 feet 6 inches and was the only carrier aircraft in an air group without folding wings. The most-produced version of the Dauntless, the SBD-5, had two forward-firing .50-caliber machine guns in the nose and twin .30-caliber flexible machine guns for the gunner, who sat behind the pilot under the greenhouse canopy. Powered by a Wright R-1820-60 Cyclone of 1,200 horsepower, the Dauntless had a cruising speed of 185 miles per hour.

TBF-1 Avenger. (U.S. Navy)

Avenger

Another Grumman product, the TBF Avenger was designed as a replacement for the aging TBD Devastator torpedo bomber and became operational just before the Hellcat. A large midwing airplane with a crew of three, the Avenger was powered by a 1,700-horsepower Wright R-2600 Cyclone and armed with one forward-firing .30-caliber machine gun in the nose cowling synchronized to fire through the propeller arc, one .50-caliber machine gun in a power-operated dorsal turret at the end of the long greenhouse canopy, and a flexible .30-caliber machine gun firing through a ventral tunnel aft of the large internal torpedo bay. Later versions of the Avenger had two forward-firing .50-caliber machine guns. The wings, which spanned 54 feet 2 inches, had to be folded back hydraulically. The Avenger was also used as a level bomber. It was a stable airplane but, although faster than its predecessor, was too slow and heavy on the controls to be used as a dive-bomber. Production was turned over to General Motors' Eastern Aircraft division; the GM-built Avenger was designated TBM. The Avenger was known affectionately by its crews as "the turkey."

INSIDE AN AIRCRAFT CARRIER

October 1943, after end of the island showing 5-inch twin mounts, quad 40-mm mounts, and Mark 37 director. (U.S. Navy)

Yorktown, a member of the *Essex* class, was over sixty feet longer, nearly ten feet greater in beam, and more than a third heavier than her predecessor. Her flight deck was longer and wider and had a rectangular outline, making takeoffs easier. The flight deck was served by three elevators, the No. 2 elevator being a deck-edge type amidships on the port side. The centerline elevators operated by hydraulic pistons, while the deck-edge elevator operated by a cable and pulley arrangement powered by a hydraulic cylinder, similar in concept to the catapults and arresting gear. The deck-edge elevator could be folded up for passage through the Panama Canal. A unique feature of the after elevator, which was offset to starboard of the centerline, was a half-platform below it, in the machinery pit. When the elevator was in the up position, this half-platform was raised to the level of the hangar deck, allowing aircraft to be moved past the pit. *Yorktown* was completed with a flight-deck catapult on the starboard side and a hangar-deck catapult as well. She was also equipped with arresting gear on the bow. The idea was that if the aft end of the flight deck was damaged, the ship could still recover aircraft by steaming astern. (In fact, high astern speed was one of the design considerations for the *Essex* class.)

Structurally, in the *Essex* class the armored hangar deck was the main strength deck and hence considered as the first (or main) deck, the deck immediately below it the second deck, then the third and fourth decks. Anything above the main deck was (and still is in modern carriers) considered superstructure, and so these decks are called "levels"—the first deck above the main deck is the 01 level, the next the 02 level, and so on. In the *Essex* class the flight deck was at the 03 level. The forecastle deck was at the 01 level, and the gallery deck, which was really only a partial deck fitted under the deep beams supporting the flight deck, was at the 02 level. The flight deck, then and now, is an aircraft carrier's reason for being. *Yorktown*'s was made of steel only 0.2 inches thick and covered with wood planking three inches thick. Metal aircraft securing rails were spaced at six-foot intervals for tying down aircraft, and where the arresting wires or barrier cables crossed the deck metal chafing plates protected the wood. The flight deck was served by three bomb elevators on the starboard side in the vicinity of the island and a torpedo elevator just behind the after 5-inch twin mount. Eight aviation gasoline (avgas) refueling stations were spaced

Mark 37 director on the forward end of the island. (U.S. Navy)

Mark 37

Two Mark 37 dual-purpose gun directors, one at each end of the island, provided fire control for the 5-inch guns against air and surface targets. The Mark 37 was gyrostabilized and equipped with a stereoscopic rangefinder. Target information was transmitted to an electromechanical computer, which calculated firing solutions (i.e., to aim the barrel from moment to moment, in lateral "train" and elevation). Introduced in the mid-1930s, it was later fitted with a Mark 4 radar, with its distinctive rectangular twin parabolic trough antenna mounted on the roof of the director. Because of the Mark 37's inability to fire in the blind (when the director crew could not see the target through optical systems), the Mark 12 radar eventually replaced the Mark 4, although it did use the same antenna. An associated height-finding radar, the Mark 22, was introduced at the same time. The Mark 22 used a small parabolic-section "orange peel" antenna mounted alongside the Mark 12 antenna. The Mark 12/22 went into ships commissioned later in the war and into many ships in 1944 during refits.

around the edges of the flight deck. They could be drained quickly and the lines flooded with inert carbon dioxide (CO_2) gas to prevent fires. This idea had first been employed by *Yorktown*'s namesake and was adopted for all later carriers.

The ship was divided into three sections, designated A (the forward section), B (the machinery spaces amidships), and C (everything aft of the machinery spaces). A compartment designated "A-0204-L," for instance, was in the forward part of the ship, on the 02 level, port side (even numbers were to port and odd numbers to starboard), and was used for crew berthing, as indicated by the suffix *L* for living space, which also included shops and offices. Other usage suffixes were *A* for supplies and storage, *C* for control, *E* for machinery, *F* for fuel, M for munitions, *T* for trunks and passageways, V for voids, and *W* for water. Below the armored fourth deck were the first and second platform decks on which were large enclosed spaces for the engine and boiler rooms, machinery rooms, ammunition and fuel storage, stores, voids, etc. Two of the 75,000 shaft-horsepower (SHP) power plants originally developed for the *Atlanta*-class light cruisers were paired in a split layout to give a total of 150,000

A 40-mm quad mount on board USS *Hornet* in action. (U.S. Navy)

40-mm Guns

The 40-mm Bofors was a Swedish design produced under license in several countries and used extensively as an antiaircraft weapon during World War II. The original was essentially redesigned for mass production; the naval versions on major ships were power operated and water-cooled, unlike the manually operated air-cooled single-barrel "army" versions used on many smaller combatants. The rate of fire was 160 rounds per minute per barrel, with an effective range of 2,500 yards (maximum about 11,000 yards) and an antiaircraft ceiling of over 22,000 feet. Each barrel was hand-fed with clips of four rounds each. From 1943 onward the Mark 51 director, essentially a manually operated Mark 14 gunsight on a pedestal mount, provided fire control. The Mark 51 directors were located as close as possible to the 40-mm guns they controlled. They could also act as directors for the 5-inch weapons.

SHP. This arrangement offered the most efficient use of space and also the best watertight subdivision and survivability.

The island, like all carrier superstructures, was cramped. It contained the main command and navigation positions, sea cabins for the senior officers, radar and radio rooms, and, of course, the boiler uptakes. The first platform above the flight deck (04 level) was the communication platform, containing the radio room, the flag (i.e., admiral's staff) office, the admiral's sea cabin, 20-mm ammunition ready-service rooms, and the aerologic office. Above the communication platform was the flag bridge (05 level) with flag plot, radar rooms, and a 40-mm ammunition ready-service room. Finally, there was the navigating bridge (06 level), where the pilothouse, captain's sea cabin, chart house, air plot, and radar rooms were located. A tripod mast forward of the funnel supported the large foremast platform on which a foretopmast pole mast was mounted. The island also mounted two Mark 37 dual-purpose gun directors, one at each end of the island, to control the fire of the 5-inch/38-caliber guns.

Radar answered the problem of carrier fighter defense, since only radar could give sufficient warning and information to allow airborne or deck-launched fighters to intercept incoming enemy aircraft. But some means of integrating its information with that from all other sources (radio and lookouts, for example) for rapid decision-making was needed. For this purpose each ship had a Combat Information Center (CIC) to sort out and keep track of the situation for the commander. Early *Essex*-class carriers had a small and cramped Radar Plot in the island structure that later became the CIC. Combat information centers were moved down to the gallery deck just below the flight deck adjacent to the island during overhauls. As part of the last generation of U.S. warships designed without major provision for radar, *Yorktown* initially carried an SK radar for long-range air search, an SG radar for surface search, and various aircraft-homing antennas, such as the YE/ZB system on the single tripod mast. Later the SK radar was moved to a sponson (cantilevered platform) on the port side of the stack, and a smaller SC radar, such as used on destroyers, was added as a backup air-search radar. All these changes were attempts to deal with mutual-interference issues and damage from stack gases to the ever-more-extensive electronic gear.

As commissioned *Yorktown* was armed with four twin 5-inch gun mounts, two forward of the island and two aft. Along the port side at the gallery-deck level were two open-mount 5-inch guns forward and two aft. There were eight 40-mm "quad" (four-barrel) mounts, Two were on the forward end of the island and two aft. One mount was on the bow, one at the stern in a small sponson offset to port, and a mount was next to each pair of the single 5-inch gun mounts on the port side at the gallery-deck level. Two mounts were later added on the starboard side aft on the hangar-deck level. There were numerous 20-mm single mounts arrayed in gun tubs around the edge of the flight deck and on the starboard side of the island. A unique feature of the *Essex* class was the positioning of radio masts along the starboard side of the flight deck with antenna wires strung between them. These masts could be rotated to a horizontal position during flight operations. *Yorktown*, like other early units, had five masts, but three masts were removed during her October 1944 refit.

5-inch Guns

In the 1930s Navy introduced the "5-inch /38," as it was known, one of the best naval weapons of World War II. (In naval parlance the "5-inch" refers to the diameter of the bore, while the "38" is the number of calibers—that is, the barrel length is 38 times five, or 190 inches.) This weapon saw service on destroyers, cruisers, battleships, and aircraft carriers, as well as on many other smaller vessels. These power-operated, dual-purpose (DP) guns were effective against not only surface targets but also air, because they could be elevated to 85 degrees and had on-mount antiaircraft (AA)–shell fuze setters. They fired semifixed ammunition—that is, the projectile and propellant cartridges were separate. Although the rounds were hand-loaded, they were power-rammed, giving the gun a high rate of fire; the gun could be easily loaded at any angle of elevation—a highly desirable quality for an antiaircraft weapon. The gun assembly itself was of the Mark 12 type used in a variety of mounts, which had their own designations. The normal rate of fire per gun was fifteen rounds per minute, but a well-trained gun crew could fire up to twenty-two rounds per minute for short periods. The maximum range for surface targets was 18,000 yards, the maximum ceiling for aircraft targets 37,000 feet. Beginning in 1943 the proximity fuse, the

Gunnery practice for *Yorktown*'s 20-mm guns, 1943. (U.S. Navy)

20-mm Guns

The 20-mm Oerlikon machine cannon was a Swiss design produced under license in large numbers. Mounted singly on a simple pedestal mount with a sixty-round drum magazine, it was aimed manually and could fire at a rate of 450 rounds per minute out to a maximum effective range of 1,000 yards. Since it operated on a simple blowback principle (similar to many submachine-gun infantry weapons) and did not require any electrical or hydraulic power, it could be put into action quickly. Because it fired explosive projectiles, which were more effective than the older .50-caliber machine-gun rounds, it was valued as a close-in weapon against attacking aircraft that got through the other defenses. The early models used ring-and-bead sights, but later versions were equipped with the Mark 14 lead-computing gyroscopic sight. The prestige it enjoyed early in the war was largely the result of its success in British use. Later in the war it proved ineffective against kamikaze attacks and began to be replaced by twin-mount versions for more firepower.

most important antiaircraft development of World War II, made the 5-inch gun a truly effective weapon against aircraft. Each round had a miniature radio transceiver with its own power supply. When the round was fired, the fuse transmitter emitted high-frequency radio waves. When a target came within effective range of the payload, the transceiver picked up the reflected waves and activated an electronic switch that initiated the detonation sequence. For security reasons, the proximity fuse was referred to as "variable time" (VT); the name "VT fuse" stuck even after its true nature was known.

The YE/ZB Homing System

The projected position of a carrier when its aircraft returned from a mission was known as "Point Option." Even with precise navigation the carrier might not be there, in which case its aircraft would have to find her. Before the war the Navy devised the YE/ZB system to help them do so. The carrier had a rotating transmitting antenna designated YE, often called the "hay rake" because of its shape, on the mainmast. Aircraft had ZB receivers with which pilots homed in on the YE beacon. The YE/ZB system had a range of about thirty miles and broadcast a different letter of the alphabet in Morse Code every 30 degrees as it rotated. From the letter heard through his headset, a pilot could approximate his bearing from the ship. The letters assigned to each "slice" changed daily; before launching, pilots filled in the day's letters on a small compass rose in the corner of their chart boards. YE/ZB was especially helpful during periods of reduced visibility and was sufficiently accurate to prevent a plane from missing a task force. Those first faint dots and dashes heard in their earphones were welcome sounds to many a lost aviator.

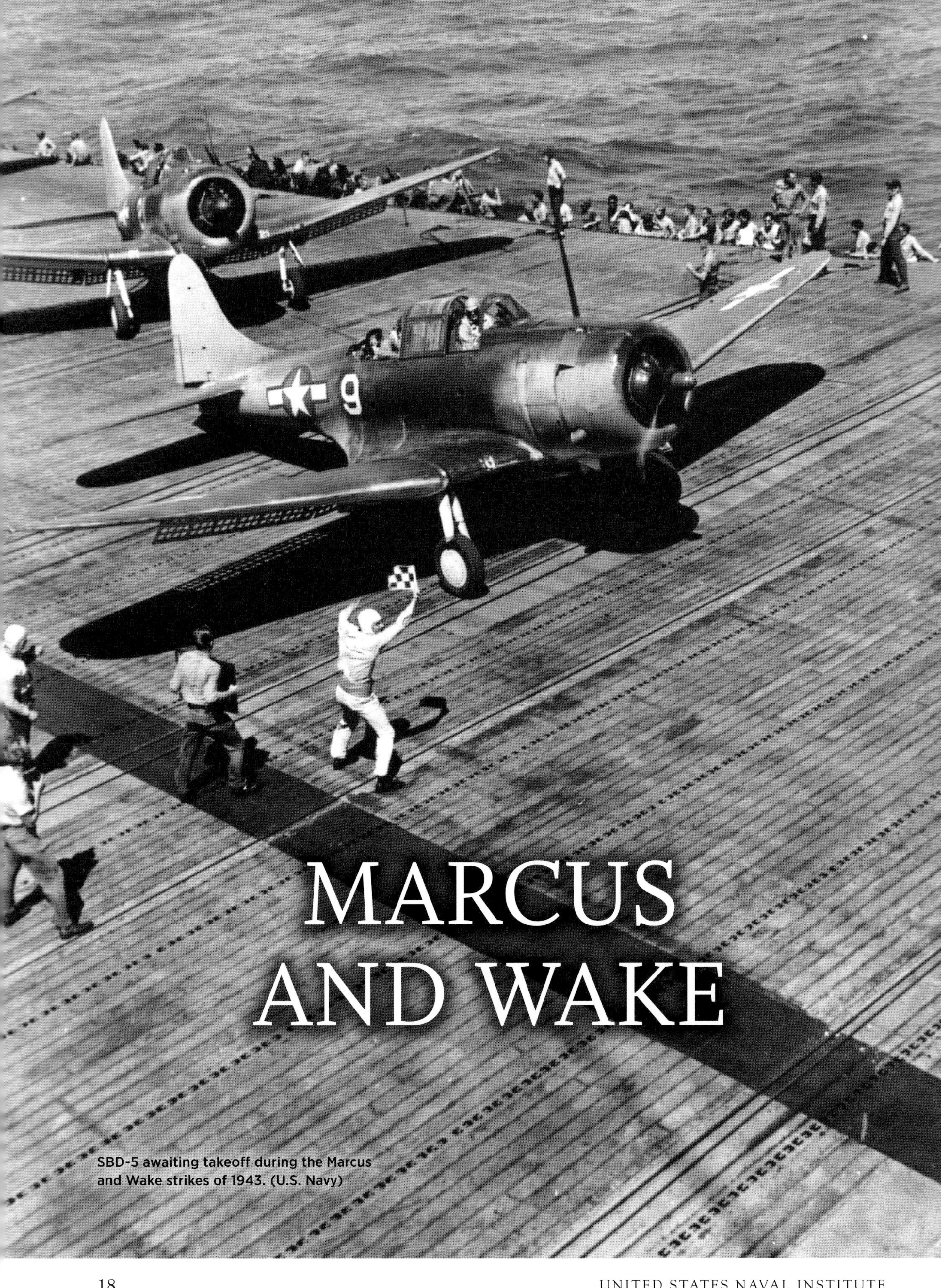

MARCUS AND WAKE

SBD-5 awaiting takeoff during the Marcus and Wake strikes of 1943. (U.S. Navy)

MARCUS

On the morning of 22 August 1943, four yard tugs eased *Yorktown* away from the dock in Pearl Harbor. A Navy band on the dock played "Aloha Oe," and *Yorktown*'s band responded with "Anchors Aweigh." The crew was mustered on the flight deck and saluted the headquarters of Adm. Chester A. Nimitz, Commander-in-Chief, Pacific Ocean Areas, as the ship moved down the channel. Three destroyers led her out to sea, followed by the light carrier *Independence* and another destroyer. As *Yorktown* passed Ford Island the tower blinked out a message, "You sure look good out there, honey!" She was on her way to her first combat operation. The target would be Marcus Island.

Marcus is 1,568 miles from Midway but less than 1,000 miles from Tokyo to the northwest. After the start of the war, the Japanese had garrisoned the island with navy and army troops and resupplied the garrison by submarine. The island would be subjected to repeated American air attacks but never captured. It was one of the targets for the American carrier raids of early 1942, and new carriers that became operational or returned from overhaul used it as a practice target. This strike was to serve as an opportunity to test out new formations and tactics for the coming Central Pacific offensives.

Task Force 15, under the command of Rear Adm. Charles A. "Baldy" Pownall, formed north of Hawaii on 23 August 1943. The task force included *Essex*, commanded by Capt. Donald B. "Wu" Duncan, with Rear Adm. Alfred E. "Monty" Montgomery on board in a learning status; the light carrier *Independence*, under Capt. George R. Fairlamb; and Jocko Clark's *Yorktown*. Rounding out the force were the fast battleship *Indiana*, two light cruisers, and ten destroyers. Pownall flew his flag in *Yorktown*. The task force was supported by a fleet oiler, and at Pownall's suggestion a submarine was standing by in the target area to pick up any downed fliers. The ships cruised in a circular formation, the three carriers in the center surrounded by the battleship and cruisers, with destroyers in an outer ring, something that had not been done previously in the war. The plan was to refuel the big ships before the strike and on retirement, and to top off the destroyers from the big ships every third or fourth day.

The second day out of Pearl Harbor Jocko Clark used what he called a "fishtail" maneuver to bring *Yorktown* back into formation after launching and recovering aircraft for the daily air patrols. This involved approaching at speed and issuing rudder commands one way and then the opposite at just the right moment to slide into position between two of the destroyers in the screen. Pownall came rushing up from the flag bridge—"Clark! Clark! Don't ever do that again!" Captain Clark was left speechless.

Commander Flatley briefs Air Group 5 pilots before the Marcus strike. (U.S. Navy)

On 27 August, after going far to the north, the task force began two days of refueling, followed a weather front all the way into the launch area. Due to a last-minute change in plans, *Yorktown*'s Air Group 5 would make the first strike. The night before Jimmy Flatley had told his pilots, "We are the best Air Group on the best ship in the Navy. Let's prove it tomorrow!"

Before dawn on 31 August, task force radars picked up a returning Japanese search plane. The task force easily followed it back to Marcus; the Japanese had not changed their patrol patterns since the carrier raids of 1942. The sea was calm and the sky clear as the big-gun

Jimmy Flatley leading Air Group 5 en route to strike Marcus, 31 August 1943. (NNAM)

"blockbuster" bombs and the SBDs 1,000-pound fragmentation "daisy cutters." Multiple runs were flown from *Yorktown*, *Essex*, and *Independence*. Flak, heavy at first, claimed three aircraft.

The submarine *Snook*, acting as "lifeguard," could not locate any of the surviving aircrew, and they were later captured. One of the aircraft lost to flak over the target was the TBF flown by Lt.

ships gave the carriers sea room while the destroyers swung out in front to mark a horizon with their lights for the pilots' reference. The carriers maneuvered at up to 30 knots, chasing any breeze, trying to give their aircraft enough wind over the deck to launch. At 0421 the first Hellcat rolled down *Yorktown*'s deck.

In the early morning hours of the gray dawn the planes caught the Japanese "with their pants down," as Pownall put it in his after-action report. On the first sweep, strafing fighters destroyed seven parked twin-engine Betty bombers, while the bombers hit the airstrip and buildings. The TBFs carried 2,000-pound

James W. "Pop" Condit. He tried to make it back to the *Yorktown*, but his Avenger gave out sixty miles north of Marcus, where he made a successful water landing. He and his crew drifted in a raft for four days until picked up by a Japanese trawler and taken prisoner. Pop Condit was eventually separated from his crew and would be one of only four *Yorktown* fliers who survived the war as prisoners of the Japanese.

The task force had closed to within ten miles of the target while rearming and refueling its aircraft, but fortunately there were no Japanese air or submarine attacks. Task Force 15 returned to Pearl Harbor on

The Crommelin Brothers

John Crommelin, the oldest of five brothers, graduated from Annapolis in 1923 and as a naval aviator earned the nickname "bomb-run John." During the war he served as air officer and XO of *Enterprise* and then chief of staff to Rear Adm. Henry M. Mullinnix on board the escort carrier *Liscome Bay* when it was torpedoed and sunk by the Japanese submarine *I-175* on 24 November 1943 during the Gilberts operation. He survived to command in 1946 the light carrier *Saipan* before being transferred to Navy headquarters in the Pentagon. There he became embroiled in the "Revolt of the Admirals" over, ostensibly, the favoring of the Air Force in defense policy. He was publicly reprimanded by the Chief of Naval Operations, Adm. Forrest P. Sherman, and then transferred to San Francisco. He retired in 1950 as a rear admiral.

Henry Crommelin, who graduated from Annapolis in 1925, originally wanted to be a naval aviator but was prevented by his poor eyesight. He served on battleships before World War II and commanded destroyers during the war, taking part in the invasion of North Africa in November 1942 as well as in operations in the Pacific. After the war he eventually became commander of the Atlantic Fleet and had attained the rank of vice admiral, the highest rank of any of the Crommelin brothers.

Charles "Charlie" Crommelin also graduated from Annapolis, in 1931. In May 1942 he was a test pilot at the naval air station at Anacostia, near downtown Washington, DC, when the engine of the aircraft he was testing failed during takeoff. He landed safely but hit a shed at the edge of the field and suffered fractures in both

8 September. Captain Fairlamb of the *Independence*, who had lost his composure during the Marcus operation, was relieved of his command when the task force returned to Pearl. Rear Admiral Pownall too had displayed nervousness and irritability; younger aviators in command of ships, up-and-coming carrier-group admirals, came to regard him as lacking in the aggressive spirit necessary to exploit fully the potential of the new fast carriers.

Following the Marcus raid Montgomery took *Essex* and *Yorktown*, escorted by four destroyers, on a "logistic mission" to San Francisco where they arrived on the 13th of September.

Aircraft carriers, with their flight decks and capacious hangars, were often used to ferry aircraft and supplies to forward areas. In San Francisco about 2,000 Army troops, hundreds of jeeps and trucks, and some Army aircraft were loaded. One of *Yorktown*'s chief petty officers, a noted "cumshaw" artist, managed to "liberate" four jeeps that would be later be used to tow aircraft and speed up the process of respotting the flight deck. (These jeeps were in addition to the small tractor "mules" the ship had previously adapted to tow aircraft.) *Yorktown* entered Pearl Harbor on the 20th.

While *Essex* and *Yorktown* were on their logistic mission, Task Force 15 with *Lexington* and the light carriers *Princeton* and *Belleau Wood* hit Tarawa on 18 September. Pownall, flying his flag in *Lexington*, again displayed nervousness and even irrationality. He would

Marcus under attack from Air Group 5. (NNAM)

Yorktown loading vehicles during her logistics mission to Alameda, 14 September 1943. (NNAM)

legs and facial abrasions. He commanded VF-5 during the attack on Marcus Island on 31 August 1943 and took over Air Group 5 from Jimmy Flatley in September. He was to be injured over Mili in November (see the next chapter) and after recovering commanded Air Group 12 on board *Randolph*. On 28 March 1945, while on temporary duty with Clark's Task Group 58.1 staff on board *Hornet*, he volunteered to fly a photographic mission over Okinawa. His Hellcat was last seen crashing offshore after a midair collision with another Hellcat in bad weather.

Richard "Dick" Crommelin served on board the old *Yorktown* and shot down two Japanese Zeros during the Coral Sea battle in May 1942. He also fought in the battle of Midway in June. Later in the war he was promoted to lieutenant commander and made the first skipper of fighter squadron VF-88 on the new *Yorktown*. He died on 14 July 1945 in a midair collision while climbing through overcast off Hokkaido with another American aircraft, a little more than three months after the loss in the same way of his brother Charlie.

Quentin Crommelin, the youngest of the five brothers, graduated from Annapolis in 1941. He survived two torpedo attacks by Japanese submarines while on board *Saratoga* before receiving orders to flight school. He flew Hellcats and Corsairs and was embarked on *Antietam* when the war ended. He retired as a captain in 1958.

SBD-5 of Bombing 5 over Wake, October 1943. (NARA)

be replaced in February 1944. After ten days in the Hawaiian Islands, during which the ship's sponsor Eleanor Roosevelt came on board for a visit, *Yorktown* returned to sea on the 29th. Also during September, Charlie Crommelin, skipper of VF-5 and now promoted to commander, relieved Jimmy Flatley as commander of Air Group 5.

WAKE

Task Force 14, under Monty Montgomery—*Essex*, *Yorktown*, *Lexington*, the light carriers *Cowpens*, *Independence*, and *Belleau Wood*, three heavy cruisers, four light cruisers, twenty-four destroyers, and two oilers—sortied from Pearl Harbor on 29 September and rendezvoused southwest of Oahu before heading for Wake Island. This was the largest fast carrier force organized up to that time; its cruisers and destroyers escorting the "heavies" would also shell the island. The task force headed due west on 1 October and on the 4th began its final run in to the target at 25 knots. The carriers launched their first strikes in the dark predawn of 5 October. At 0445 *Yorktown* began launching a dozen Hellcats and a half-dozen Avengers; a radar-equipped Avenger guided them toward Wake, 90 miles to the south. For the first time enemy fighters were met over the target, but the Hellcats shot down most of the defending Zeros. Weather delayed the launching of the second strike until 0537. This was a full-deckload strike, Hellcats, Dauntlesses, and Avengers, led by Charlie Crommelin to hit a rain-soaked Wake.

This strike too encountered airborne Zeros; when the Hellcats were not tangling with the Zeros or covering the bombers they went down to strafe. One bomber went missing, but no fighters or torpedo planes were lost.

Another strike was launched to hit Wake, again with combat air patrols (CAPs) over the island, as well as the usual antisubmarine (ASW) patrols. The weather was even worse the next day, when the attacks and patrols were repeated.

Two Dauntlesses collided in a rainsquall and were seen falling into the sea in flames. One Hellcat crashed on the runway on Wake, another was seen spinning into a cloud over Wake but not seen again, and a third made a forced landing in the sea north of Wake. The pilot managed to set down near the submarine *Skate*, assigned to lifeguard duty off Wake. *Skate* herself was strafed at dawn on the 6th by a Japanese plane, seriously wounding one of her officers, who later died. She then moved up to about six miles off the reefs but was forced to submerge by fire from a Japanese coast-defense gun. Nevertheless, *Skate* managed to rescue six aircrew. The morale of all carrier airmen was greatly enhanced by knowing that the "lifeguard league" submarines were standing by to rescue them.

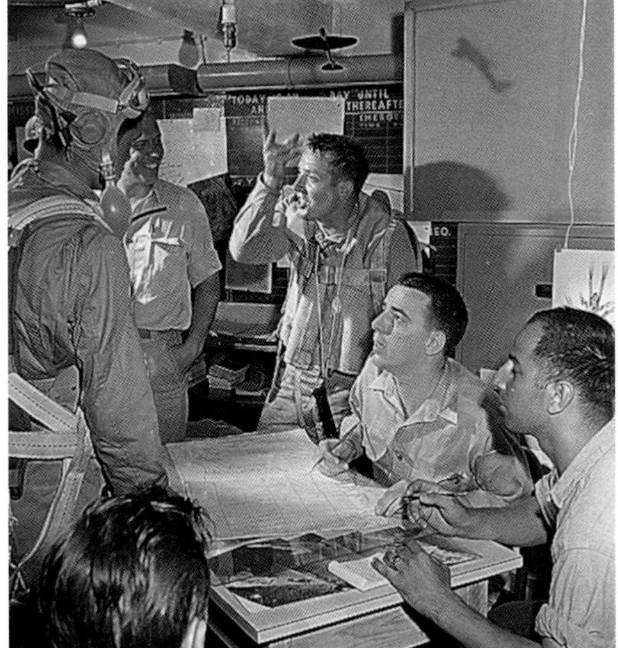

(top left) Pilots debriefing in a ready room following the Wake strikes. (U.S. Navy)

(top right) Charlie Crommelin, commander of Air Group 5, on the wing of his Hellcat, September 1943. (U.S. Navy)

(left) Captain Clark and Rear Admiral Radford on the open bridge, 1943. Radford would be *Yorktown*'s first and last admiral of the war. (U.S. Navy)

The task group retired to Hawaii that evening. *Yorktown* arrived at Oahu on the 11th and for the next month conducted air training out of Pearl Harbor. During this period Air Group 5, which had routinely moved to the air station ashore, flew out to make night carrier-qualification landings and takeoffs to avoid repeating problems experienced in the predawn launches at Marcus and Wake. During the planning for a gunnery training exercise with *Yorktown*, *Lexington*, and five destroyers under Rear Admiral Pownall, Admiral Nimitz suggested that *Yorktown* shoot at the target drone first. Jocko Clark, immensely proud of his gun crews, responded, "Admiral, suppose the five destroyers fire at the drone first, then the *Lexington*, then *I'll* [emphasis supplied] shoot it down." And so it happened: when the ships sortied from Pearl Harbor on the 15th, the five destroyers fired at the drone followed by the *Lexington*. Pownall then invited *Yorktown* to take its turn, after which *Lexington* would try again, but Clark responded, "Admiral, if you allow us to shoot at the drone there will be no drone left for the *Lexington* to shoot at." Pownall passed this off, but *Yorktown* indeed brought down the drone with its first salvo. The ships returned to Pearl Harbor on the 17th.

GALVANIC

On 10 November 1943, *Yorktown* departed Pearl Harbor as part of Task Force 50, the Fast Carrier Force, to participate in Operation Galvanic, the occupation of the Gilbert Islands. It would be the first major assault operation of the Central Pacific Force (to become the Fifth Fleet in April 1944) under Vice Adm. Raymond A. Spruance, who had risen to command it after leading Task Force 16 in the battle of Midway. The assault forces assembled for Galvanic included the Northern Attack Force, Task Force 52, commanded by Rear Adm. Richmond K. "Terrible" Turner and headed for Makin, and the Southern Attack Force, Task Force 53, commanded by Rear Adm. Harry W. Hill and bound for Tarawa. The Fast Carrier Force was itself divided into four task groups, each with its own mission. The Carrier Interceptor Group, Task Group 50.1, was commanded by Rear Admiral Pownall in *Yorktown* and included the new *Lexington* and the light carrier *Cowpens*. The Northern Carrier Group, TG 50.2, commanded by Rear Adm. Arthur W. "Raddy" Radford in *Enterprise*, also included the light carriers *Belleau Wood* and *Monterey*. The Southern Carrier Group, Task Group 50.3, under Rear Admiral Montgomery in *Essex*, included *Bunker Hill* and the light carrier *Independence*. The Relief

Spotting SBD-5 bombers for takeoff 20 November 1943 for Marshalls strikes in support of the Gilberts landings. (U.S. Navy)

Carrier Group, Task Group 50.4, Rear Adm. Frederick C. "Ted" Sherman, included the old *Saratoga* and the light carrier *Princeton*. Both of these latter task groups had been lent to the South Pacific and had sent several strikes into Rabaul between 1 and 11 November.

While en route with Task Group 50.1, *Yorktown* launched antisubmarine, combat air, and sector search patrols. Air Group 5 also made simulated air attacks on the formation, and its Avengers would tow target sleeves for the ships to practice their gunnery. The run-in to the target began on the 17th. On the 19th, *Yorktown* and her task group arrived at the launch point near Jaluit and Mili in the southern Marshalls. Early that morning she launched the first of a series of raids to hit Japanese airfields during the amphibious assaults on Tarawa, Abemama, and Makin.

The next day she sent raids to the airfield on Jaluit for the second straight day and also provided support for the troops taking Makin.

On 21 November Commander Crommelin was leading a reconnaissance flight over Mili Atoll with seven other Hellcats. As he and his wingman, Lt. (jg) Murray Tyler, approached the islet he spotted two planes on its airstrip taxiing to take off. He ordered the rest of the aircraft to stay clear. On his and Tyler's first run, at medium altitude, he strafed a Nell and a group of trucks. His second pass was made from the opposite direction at lower altitude so as to strafe a Betty on the runway that he had spotted on the first pass. As he made a slight left turn out of the second pass Japanese antiaircraft guns opened up, and he was turning right to head for cloud cover when a 20-mm explosive shell hit his windscreen, exploding fragments into the cockpit. Temporarily blinded, he leveled off, shaking his head to clear his vision and found he could see out of his left eye but not his right. He knew he'd been hit from the pain in his head, right leg, and right wrist. He passed to Tyler that he had been hit, and

Checking bomb fuses before loading them on *Yorktown*'s planes, 20 November 1943. (U.S. Navy)

Charlie Crommelin's Hellcat back on board *Yorktown* after being hit over Mili, 21 November 1943. (U.S. Navy)

they rendezvoused west of the island to head back to *Yorktown*, more than a hundred miles away. Flying with his left hand, he tried to make a tourniquet with his right hand to stop the bleeding on that hand. He realized that loss of blood might make him too weak to recover on board *Yorktown*, so he prepared for a water landing by releasing his belly tank, loosening the straps on his parachute and finding his life raft. Tyler passed the word to *Yorktown*, where every crew member who could leave his post climbed to where he could witness the recovery. After circling once, Crommelin's damaged Hellcat made a perfect landing. He even taxied out of the arresting gear before stopping. Corpsmen carried him to sick bay, where fragments and bits of debris were removed from his body.

Lt. Cdr. Edgar E. Stebbins, skipper of VB-5, would take over command of Air Group 5 for the next series of operations. (Since he had not been checked out in the Hellcat, Jocko Clark arranged for him to take off in one from *Yorktown* on the afternoon of the 24th. After circling the ship a few times Stebbins made a perfect landing, reassuring everyone that he was ready to lead the air group.)

On 22 November Air Group 5 hit installations and planes at Mili again and maintained a combat air patrol over the task group.

On the evening of the 23rd a storm came up, and four Wildcats from *Liscome Bay*, one of the escort carriers providing close air support for the Army troops ashore on Makin, asked for permission to land on *Yorktown*. The first three aircraft got onto the deck safely, but the last did not—the pilot had forgotten to lower his tailhook. The aircraft bounced, and the pilot tried to go around, managing to clear the barricade wires (which protected planes parked forward). But the Wildcat slammed back down onto the flight deck and its belly tank ruptured and exploded, setting fire to ammunition and flares stored in the parked aircraft. The pilot managed to squirm free as the flames spread. As the damage-control parties rushed to smother the flames, Captain Clark kept *Yorktown* into the wind to keep the fire from spreading forward. Meanwhile, the air officer ordered other planes waiting to land on *Yorktown* to *Lexington* instead. Gasoline spilled down to the hangar deck, and there were some anxious moments until the fires were brought under control some fourteen minutes later. Five aircraft were destroyed and five crewmen killed, but by the next morning *Yorktown* was again operational. The two task groups departed the area around Tarawa on the night of 27–28 November, refueling on 1 December.

Pownall was ordered to detach *Bunker Hill* and *Monterey* from his TG 50.1 and leave them north of the Gilberts under Sherman. The remainder (*Yorktown*, *Lexington*, and *Cowpens*) and Montgomery's Task Group 50.3 (reshuffled to include *Essex*, *Enterprise*, and *Belleau Wood*) were to hit Kwajalein, in the Marshalls.

The force approached the target from the northeast on 4 December. *Yorktown* bombed and strafed installations on Kwajalein and on Wotje, another Marshalls atoll about 185 miles east, But the results were poor. As the strikes returned they spotted many Bettys on an airfield on nearby Roi-Namur, but Pownall would not launch a second strike. About noon, two flights of four Kate torpedo bombers each attacked the task force just as the strike on Wotje was launching.

Lexington, off *Yorktown*'s starboard bow, shot down three Kates that had attacked her, all their torpedoes passing astern. At 1240 *Yorktown* began landing her combat air patrol. Minutes later *Yorktown* and the heavy cruiser *San Francisco* off her port beam opened fire on three Kates attacking from off *Yorktown*'s port bow.

Looking aft on the flight deck during the Marshalls–Gilberts operations. (U.S. Navy)

As the range closed *Yorktown* gunners kept lowering their aim until they were shooting into *San Francisco*. As one Kate pressed its attack Pownall yelled up to Clark, "Cease fire! Cease fire! You are firing at that cruiser!" Clark ignored the order and his gunners brought down the last Kate, to fall close astern on the starboard side.

After recovering the Wotje strike, Task Force 50 headed for friendly waters, but heavy seas slowed it down. Everyone knew the Japanese would make night torpedo attacks. Jocko Clark several times pounded the *Yorktown*'s chart desk with his fist, exclaiming, "Goddammit, you can't run away from airplanes with ships!" Steaming at 18 knots, Task Force 50 prepared for a night attack. It came, under a bright moon, shortly after 2000. Thirty to fifty Bettys, guided by "snooper" aircraft that had shadowed the task force, attacked. The task force broke up into two task groups; Pownall's group relied on independent evasive ship maneuvers and antiaircraft fire. (The carrier task

***Yorktown*'s hangar deck during the Marshalls–Gilberts operations. (U.S. Navy)**

Japanese Kates attacking *Yorktown* during the raids on the Marshalls, as seen from *Lexington*, 4 December 1943. (U.S. Navy)

forces had no night-fighter capability at this point in the war.) Captain Stump of the *Lexington*, more charitable to Pownall than Jocko Clark, felt afterward that the course changes had saved the task force from a coordinated attack. The attack was erratic, sometimes heavy, sometimes only threatening. Like her namesake the year before, *Lexington* was hit by a torpedo, which knocked her out of the war until full repairs were made. The last attack was beaten off by the ships' fire and hindered by the increasing darkness, which became complete at moonset around 0130 on 5 December.

Yorktown reentered Pearl Harbor on 9 December and began a month of air training operations in the Hawaiian Islands. The next objective for the Central Pacific Force would be the Marshalls, on which would be established logistics facilities critical to sustaining the advance across the Pacific. The Marshalls, an archipelago of coral atolls hundreds of miles across, includes Kwajalein, with the world's largest lagoon.

A Kate explodes after a direct hit by a 5-inch shell off Kwajalein, 4 December 1943. *Life* magazine featured this photograph in full page, and it became famous as the "Flaming Kate." (U.S. Navy)

A Japanese torpedo bomber splashes off *Yorktown*'s starboard side during the Gilbert Islands operations, 4 December 1943. (NHHC)

FLINTLOCK

On 13 January 1944, Rear Adm. Marc A. "Pete" Mitscher hoisted his flag in *Yorktown* as commander of Task Force 58, the Fast Carrier Force of the Pacific Fleet. Mitscher would lead the fast carriers in the drive across the Central Pacific. An early naval aviator, Mitscher had been the captain of the old *Hornet* during the Doolittle Tokyo raid in April 1942 and at the battle of Midway that June. After the loss of *Hornet* at the battle of Santa Cruz, he took over as Adm. William F. "Bull" Halsey Jr.'s land-based air commander in the Solomons. Quiet and soft-spoken, Mitscher held the respect of all his carrier group commanders. He was always ready to give his carrier commanders their heads if they performed—"I tell them what I want done, not how."

On the 16th *Yorktown* left Pearl Harbor to support Operation Flintlock, the amphibious assault on the Marshalls. As part of Task Group 58.1, under Rear Adm. John W. "Black Jack" Reeves, in company with *Lexington* and *Cowpens*, she arrived at the launching point early on the morning of 29 January and sending air strikes against Taroa airfield on Maloelap. Throughout the day *Yorktown*'s aircraft hit Maloelap in preparation for the assaults on Majuro and Kwajalein scheduled for the 31st. Late that afternoon the destroyers in the screen opened fire on low-flying aircraft that turned out to be Army B-25s, which were also attacked by the combat air patrol before they were identified as friendly. One B-25 was shot down and crashed about six miles ahead of the formation, but a destroyer rescued the surviving crew members. *Yorktown* and her planes did not participate in the

Captain Clark congratulates Capt. Ralph Jennings on his assuming command of *Yorktown*, 10 February 1944. (NHHC)

misdirected firing, but this did not help the mood on board as four Avengers had been lost—one crashing on takeoff during the first launch (although the crew was rescued by a destroyer), one shot down by flak over the target, and two missing.

While Task Group 58.1 was hitting Maloelap, Montgomery's Task Group 58.2 attacked the airfield on Roi, Task Group 58.3 under Ted Sherman hit Kwajalein, and Rear Adm. Samuel P. "Cy" Ginder's Task Group 58.4 bombed Wotje. On the 30th, *Yorktown* and her sister carriers shifted targets to Kwajalein to begin softening up one of the objectives of the assault. When the troops landed on Kwajalein on the 31st, her aviators continued their strikes in their support. (Kwajalein and Roi-Namur were secured by 7 February, after which "mopping-up" lasted a few days.) Her Air Group 5 continued this support during the first three days in February. On the 4th, the task group retired to the fleet anchorage at recently secured Majuro, 2,000 miles west of Pearl Harbor.

The string of islets forming Majuro Atoll, in the center of the triangle formed by Jaluit, Maloelap, and Mili, encloses a lagoon 21 miles long and six to eight miles wide. Japan had stationed troops there when the war began but had sent them to Mili before the Allies landed on the 31st. It was soon developed into an advanced naval and air base. Commercial tankers carrying bulk fuel to transfer to Navy oilers could bypass Hawaii, cutting down transit times to the forward area. Fleet tankers, from which combatants could refuel alongside at anchor, arrived in Majuro soon after its occupation, reducing the need for at-sea refueling during the Marshalls operations. Two airfields were soon operational, and from them land-based aircraft pounded Mili, Maloelap, and Wotje, preventing air attacks on the anchorage. The fast carriers would put in to Majuro between strikes, increasing the pace of operations in the Central Pacific. The departure of Task Force 58 from Pearl Harbor late that January had marked the last time the fast carriers would operate from Hawaii, which had become a rear area. While most of Task Force 58 enjoyed a brief lull at Majuro, Jocko Clark was promoted to rear admiral and became commander, Carrier Division 13 (ComCarDiv13), and Capt. Ralph E. Jennings relieved him in command of *Yorktown* on the 10th. In contrast to the fiery Jocko Clark, Ralph Jennings was a man of quiet efficiency who tolerated errors on the part of his officers but would counsel them and encourage them to greater performance. He was to be remembered as a gentleman who never lost his composure during the tensest of situations. He would lead *Yorktown* during the Truk strikes, the campaign to occupy the Marianas, and in the battle of the Philippine Sea.

After eight days at Majuro, on 12 February, *Yorktown* sortied with her task group to participate in Operation Hailstone, the strike on the main Japanese anchorage at Truk.

Crossing the Line

War or no war, some seafaring traditions were upheld as *Yorktown* headed for the Marshalls. On 21 January 1944 she crossed both the equator and the international date line, and the nearly 3,000 lowly pollywogs on board became both shellbacks and dragonbacks (whereas pollywogs who cross the equator at the Greenwich meridian become "golden shellbacks") in the time-honored rites of passage for seafarers. As is also traditional, the planning meeting of the shellbacks the evening before was set upon by a group of pollywogs, who soaked every shellback with hoses. The offending pollywogs would pay for their audacity the next day. After the usual gunnery exercises all work was knocked off, and except for watch standers everyone went to quarters on the flight deck to await the arrival of Davy Jones and King Neptune's royal party, all dressed in appropriately outlandish costumes. Davy Jones ascended to the bridge to read the indictment of the pollywogs for violating King Neptune's realm. A group of shellback aviators in full flight gear ran around the flight deck simulating takeoff and landing. Another group, this time fighter-pilot pollywogs, retaliated by "strafing" the shellbacks with Navy beans. The other pollywogs were in outlandish costumes as well and were subjected to various indignities that involved crawling through noxious mixtures, enduring painful whacks from paddles, as well as receiving "haircuts" from the Royal Barber. But the new shellbacks would have to "turn to" quickly as *Yorktown* prepared to strike her first targets in the Marshalls.

TRUK

Located to the west of the Marshalls in the center of the Carolines, Truk was regarded as the "Gibraltar of the Pacific." The Japanese had militarily built up Truk in secrecy since the 1930s, and there were serious misgivings among the aircrews when they learned they were to attack it. Mitscher headed for Truk with three task groups, topping off from five tankers before making a high-speed run into the target area, while Ginder's Task Group 58.4 was left behind to cover the Eniwetok landings, Operation Catchpole. In the first week of February a Marine PB4Y Liberator had flown a long-range photo reconnaissance mission over Truk from Bougainville and found numerous enemy warships anchored in the lagoon, though low-lying clouds prevented complete coverage. Alerted by this overflight, the Japanese withdrew the majority of their warships to Palau before the raids began on 17 February.

Task Force 58 was well at sea before anyone learned where they were bound. The air group commanders flew to *Yorktown*, Mitscher's flagship, for a conference and returned to their carriers to pass the word. When Lt. Cdr. Phil Torrey, the Air Group 9 skipper in *Essex*, heard the announcement, his first instinct, he later admitted, was to jump overboard. As the task force approached the launch point, apprehension gradually wore off. Lt. Cdr. Ed Owen, skipper of VF-5, would recall,

"By D-Day I think everyone was a tiger." Mitscher tried some new tactics for the Truk strikes, including tightening task group formations and following rain squalls on the way into the launch area. Also, as had recently become possible, the carriers had specially equipped night-fighter detachments to counter the possibility of attacks on the task force in the hours of darkness. The four night Hellcats on *Yorktown* were from VF(N)-76 Detachment B. They would be spotted on the catapults for immediate launch if needed. On the afternoon of the 14th the CAP from *Belleau Wood* was vectored out to an unidentified air contact picked up on radar by the *Enterprise*. It turned out to be a Betty and was shot down still out of sight of the task force. The next day the task force began its high-speed run in to the target.

An hour and a half before dawn, the task force reached the launch point 100 miles northeast of Truk.

Japanese shipping under air attack in Truk Lagoon on the first day of raids, 17 February 1944. Dublon Island is at left, Moen in the background. Four ships have been hit. (U.S. Navy)

The first aircraft off would comprise the fighter sweep of Hellcats to clear the area of Japanese aircraft that might interfere with the bombers. *Bunker Hill*'s VF-18 provided high cover at 20,000 feet; *Enterprise*'s VF-10, *Intrepid*'s VF-6, *Essex*'s VF-9, and *Yorktown*'s VF-5 also contributed. The fighter squadrons on board the light carriers *Belleau Wood*, *Cowpens*, *Monterey*, and *Cabot* remained with the task force to provide combat air patrol and act as a reserve. (This became a standard practice and was a sore point among the light carrier squadrons.)

Lt. Cdr. William "Killer" Kane from *Enterprise* led the dozen Hellcats from VF-10 and a dozen from *Intrepid*'s VF-6 to a rendezvous at 1,500 feet, then swung around to approach the atoll from the north for the final run-in, maintaining an altitude of about 1,000 feet halfway to the target before they began climbing for the attack. VF-5 approached well below, while the *Bunker Hill* fighters were at altitude, almost out of sight. The sun was not yet up when Kane's fighters arrived over the lagoon at 13,000 feet. After circling Moen Island the Hellcats dove to strafe the airfield. The Japanese, caught by surprise, scrambled fighters only minutes before the sweep arrived and managed to scramble more during the ensuing action but many were destroyed on the ground.

As the dawn fighter sweep erupted into the largest dogfight most of the pilots had ever been in, the rising sun tinted the clouds with reddish hues. As VF-5's skipper Ed Owen later recalled, "Jap airplanes were burning and falling from every quarter, and many were crashing on takeoff as a result of strafing them on the ground. Ground installations were exploding and burning, and all this in the early golden glow of dawn. At times it might have been staged for the movies."

Lt. Robert Duncan led VF-5's scoring for the day with four kills. His division was flying cover for *Yorktown*'s 1300 strike when he spotted 10 to 15 Zeros attacking out of the sun from 20,000 feet. The *Yorktown* Hellcats, 6,000 feet below, went into defensive weaves. One Zero made a pass at Duncan's section from ten o'clock high; he and his wingman turned into the Zero, although his wingman's Hellcat was hit. As the Zero passed overhead, Duncan turned back after it and shot it down with a long burst. A second Zero suddenly appeared ahead of Duncan, who fired but missed. This Zero then turned to face him and Duncan fired again as it passed, setting it on fire. His third kill was a Zero whose pilot

The Moen Island seaplane base and shipping burning. The airfield is in the lower center, Dublon Island upper left center, Eten Island airfield just beyond. Fefan Island is at right. (U.S. Navy)

was evidently more experienced. The two "scissored" against each other, each attempting to cause the other to overshoot and make himself vulnerable, but neither pilot could gain an advantage. Eventually the Japanese pilot broke off; Duncan dove after him and sent him down in flames. His port guns now jammed, Duncan climbed to 8,000 feet when a fourth Zero made a run on him, about 300 feet above. This Zero rolled inverted and closed in on what appeared to be a suicide attempt. Duncan pulled up sharply after firing his starboard guns and banked around for another shot, but the Zero was slowly spiraling down to crash into the hills on Dublon, the pilot apparently killed during his head-on run. (Bob Duncan had been the first Hellcat pilot to down a Zero when he shot down a pair of them during the Wake Island raid of early October 1943. His victories over Truk brought his score to seven Zeros.)

Four other VF-5 pilots accounted for another ten kills during the day, including the skipper, Ed Owen, who got two, and Lt. (jg) Tom McClelland, who shot down three. Lt. (jg) Teddy Schofield also shot down two. His second opponent attempted a forced landing, but his Zero caught the ground with one wing and cartwheeled into a row of torpedo planes before careening over three hills, setting them afire, and coming to a halt only yards from a big four-engine aircraft. *Yorktown*'s air group commander, Edgar Stebbins, became an ace over Truk flying a camera-equipped Hellcat. He was attacked by a lone Zero and shot it down. (Stebbins had shot down three planes as an SBD pilot on board the old *Hornet* in 1942 and had splashed a Betty bomber off Kwajalein in December.) Another pilot, now flying from *Essex* but later serving on *Yorktown*, also had an exciting day. VF-9's Lt. (jg) Eugene A. Valencia scored three kills, raising him to ace status on his way to becoming the Navy's third-highest-scoring fighter pilot.

All this damage was in exchange for four Hellcats. One of them was piloted by Lt. Elisha T. "Smokey" Stover. Smokey was a veteran fighter pilot who been on the old *Hornet* at Midway and had flown out of Henderson Field on Guadalcanal before returning stateside for assignment to the *Yorktown*.

As a qualified pilot he was assigned to Radar Plot, later CIC, where his expertise would be invaluable, but longed to get back to flying and was reassigned to VF-5. Over Truk, on the first day of strikes, his Hellcat was hit by

The airfield on Eten from a *Yorktown* plane. A large number of Japanese planes are on the field, and numerous bomb craters are visible. Dublon Island is in the background, at the top. (U.S. Navy)

antiaircraft fire and caught fire. He managed to bail out three miles beyond the reef and was last seen in his rubber raft. But the prevailing wind drove him toward the North Pass, through which Japanese warships were trying to escape the attack. After the war it was learned that Smokey had been executed along with six other downed aviators whose rafts had also been stranded on the reef. (Maj. Greg "Pappy" Boyington, the highest-scoring Marine ace, had been shot down over Rabaul the month before and taken prisoner. He was on Truk on his way to a prisoner of war camp in Japan when the raid began, and he witnessed the attack firsthand. He had flown with his friend Pop Condit on the old *Yorktown* before the war; the two would be held in the same camp in Japan and remain in touch after the war.)

Smokey Stover on the wing of his Hellcat. He would be shot down over Truk and executed along with six other survivors of the attack. (U.S. Navy)

By the afternoon no Japanese fighters challenged the raid. Following the fighter sweep came Avengers loaded with fragmentation clusters and incendiaries with which to hit the aircraft dispersal areas. Strike planning incorporated a number of innovations. One was staggering the launch of strike aircraft so that there were attackers over the target almost continuously. Also, delayed-action 1,000-pound bombs would be used on the last runway strikes to make repair during the night more difficult. Finally, strikes against oil storage sites were saved for last, to keep the flame and smoke from obscuring other targets. Many attacks were directed at the Japanese shipping in the lagoon; waiting U.S. submarines set upon targets that managed to escape. An Avenger damaged over the target came back to recover on board that afternoon with two wounded enlisted crewmen, one of whom died of his wounds.

Vice Admiral Spruance, now commander of the Fifth Fleet, personally assumed command of Task Force 50, shifting his flag to the new battleship *New Jersey* in order to participate in a surface engagement during the attack. Spruance led an "around-the-atoll cruise" to catch escaping Japanese ships, bombarding shore installations as it went.

That night small groups of "bogies" (unidentified air contacts) appeared on task force radars; the Japanese were out looking for the attacking carriers. *Yorktown* launched a night fighter to drive off the snoopers, but a small group of radar-equipped Japanese Kates moved in on *Intrepid*. Ships' gunfire drove off most, but one got through and scored a torpedo hit on *Intrepid*'s starboard side aft below the waterline, taking her out of the war for months. Between midnight and dawn Mitscher launched the first night attack on shipping of the war with radar-equipped Avengers from *Enterprise*. At dawn on the 18th, aircraft from *Enterprise*, *Yorktown*, *Essex*, and *Bunker Hill* attacked Truk again. They met no air opposition and bombed and strafed airfields, hangars, storage tanks, and ammo dumps. A *Yorktown* Avenger landed in the water near the target, but the crew was rescued by the lifeguard submarine.

The attack on Truk marked a change in how the fast carriers operated. Previous American carrier raids had been "hit and run" affairs, owing to the prewar assumption that aircraft carriers could not survive within range of strong land-based air opposition. Truk proved that this was no longer true. The Japanese would never again use Truk as a major naval base; it would be bypassed as the war in the Pacific moved on.

PACIFIC RAIDS

The Marianas stretch from southeast of Iwo Jima in a rough arc down to Guam, north of the Carolines. The four biggest islands—Saipan, Tinian, Rota, and Guam—are all at the southern end of the chain. Following the Truk strike, Task Force 58 stayed at sea, replenishing under way on 19 February before moving on to strike the Marianas. (Spruance himself had returned to Majuro.) With the departure of *Intrepid* and *Cabot* and later *Enterprise*, the task groups were reshuffled. Montgomery's Task Group 58.2 now included *Yorktown*, *Essex*, and *Belleau Wood*, while Task Group 58.3 comprised *Bunker Hill*, *Monterey*, and *Cowpens*.

In the evening of 21 February the task force went into an air-defense formation in anticipation of Japanese night attacks, and as unidentified aircraft were picked up on radar *Yorktown* went to General Quarters and her task group executed a series of successive turns to avoid the incoming planes. After about an hour some ships in the formation opened fire but apparently did not hit anything. Minutes later a glow on the horizon off *Yorktown*'s port quarter was seen, apparently a plane shot down by Task Group 58.3. A plane closed on Task Group 58.2; the screen opened fire, and it crashed in the water and burned. No other planes approached for about fifteen minutes, and when another came in it was driven off by gunfire. Just before midnight the task group was attacked again, and that plane was also shot down. A half hour past midnight two other planes were shot down. One more attack was made that lasted thirty minutes, during which four more attackers were brought down. At dawn radar picked up another contact in the vicinity. It was a Betty that at 0808 made a run on the formation but was driven off. Task Force 58 had been detected, but Mitscher was undeterred, saying, "We'll fight our way in."

Yorktown began launching her first strike against Saipan at 0814. For the next hour and a half the Japanese sent torpedo attacks against the formation, but few got within torpedo range. The screen shot down three Bettys, and the CAP shot down two Nells. A fighter, thought to be a Tony, dived on the *Essex* and released its bomb before flying through the formation. A few minutes later a twin-engine plane, possibly a Nick, dove on *Yorktown*, but automatic-weapons fire, 20- and 40-mm, forced the pilot to release his bomb early and pull out of his dive too high. The bomb fell about a hundred yards off the starboard bow. Another plane dived on the *Essex* and was shot down after releasing its bomb.

Yorktown, 100 miles from Saipan and Tinian, continued to launch strikes throughout the morning

Japanese torpedo bomber flying through hail of anti-aircraft fire toward *Yorktown* during Truk Island raid. (U.S. Naval Institute photo archive)

and afternoon. Most of the intercepting aircraft were shot down. A new airfield on Guam was discovered and attacked; many Japanese aircraft were destroyed and several transports sunk. Two *Yorktown* Hellcats went missing over the target from unknown causes.

Task Force 58 headed for Majuro on 22 February, unlocated by Japanese snoopers. *Yorktown* arrived in Majuro Lagoon on the 26th and remained there, resting and replenishing, before getting under way on the 28th with *Enterprise* and *Belleau Wood* to exchange aircraft before returning to Majuro. On 8 March *Yorktown* stood out of Majuro once again, rendezvoused with Task Group 58.4, and headed for Espiritu Santo in the New Hebrides, where she arrived on the 13th and remained for ten days. *Yorktown* then got under way again to rendezvous with the rest of Task Force 58, which had sortied from Majuro, becoming part of Task Group 58.3. Heading for Palau in the western Carolines, Task Force 58 swung south to avoid Truk-based search aircraft but was spotted on the 25th. Thus alerted, the Japanese withdrew their fleet units to Singapore, Borneo, and Japanese home waters. On

Helldivers with the white stripe on the vertical fin worn by *Yorktown*'s air group. (NHHC)

The Helldiver

The Curtiss SB2C Helldiver was a mediocre dive-bomber that never lived up to expectations. It was eventually supplanted by other types of aircraft, although many of its early faults were corrected in later versions. The Helldiver was a large aircraft whose wings and tail seemed disproportionately large compared to its fuselage. Like the Avenger, the Helldiver was powered by the R-2600 Cyclone. It was armed with two 20-mm cannon in the wings and twin .30-caliber machine guns for the rear gunner. The early Helldiver design exhibited poor stability and low-speed handling characteristics; later modifications lengthened the fuselage and increased the area of the tail surfaces to correct these problems. The design of the dive flaps caused buffeting, degrading accuracy. Finally, it was a difficult aircraft to operate from a carrier. All in all, the Helldiver performed no better than the SBD-5 Dauntless dive-bombers except for a marginal increase in speed and heavier forward-firing armament. It was nicknamed "the beast" by its crews, a title it fully deserved. *Yorktown*'s dive-bomber squadrons were equipped with the initial operational version of the Helldiver, the SB2C-1, from May through June 1943 during her shakedown cruise. They suffered from many mechanical problems, including a tendency of the tailhooks to pull out during landings. Captain Clark refused to take them into combat and had them replaced with SBD-5s. Later, improved versions did serve on board *Yorktown*, beginning with VB-1.

the 29th the Japanese made night torpedo attacks. As the task force's run-in to the target began, its ASW patrol reported a Betty forty miles distant. Fighters were vectored out and soon reported the Betty shot down. Another Betty was shot down twelve miles west of Yorktown's task group. Radar then picked up unidentified aircraft to the northwest, which formed three groups and began to close the task group, which made emergency turns. The attackers continued to close. The screen opened fire at the nearest ones; minutes later two burst into flames and crashed on either quarter of *Yorktown*. At dawn on 30 March, Task Force 58 launched a fighter sweep from ninety miles south of the target, Palau, eliminating the airborne Zeros. The fighters then joined the bombers in attacking merchant shipping there. Torpedoes sank a Japanese destroyer, and Avengers from *Lexington*, *Bunker Hill*, and *Hornet* mined Palau's waters. (This turned out to be the first and only time mines were dropped by planes from the fast carriers during the war. It proved to be too dangerous for the low and slow Avengers and was left to long-range land-based bombers thereafter.)

That night, more enemy aircraft flew into Palau, and on 31 March Task Groups 58.2 and 58.3 hit Palau again while TG 58.1 hit Yap to the northeast. All three task groups hit Wolei on 1 April. A few aircraft visited Ulithi, northeast of Yap, but found few targets—most were on Palau. Along with dozens of aircraft shot down, the Japanese lost about 130,000 tons of shipping to bombing and delayed-action mines. On the American side, of 44 aircrew ditching at sea, 26 were picked up by submarines, seaplanes, and destroyers. Five days later Task Force 58 returned to Majuro for a week's rest and replenishment before departing to support the next major amphibious assault, this time in New Guinea.

HOLLANDIA

The Hollandia operation briefly brought together the Nimitz's Central Pacific and MacArthur's Southwest Pacific forces. Having neutralized Japanese air forces in the Palaus, Task Force 58 provided close air support for MacArthur's Hollandia landings on 22 April. MacArthur's air commander, Gen. George Kenny, had already on 30 March and 3, 5, and 12 April sent massive land-based air attacks that had largely eliminated Hollandia

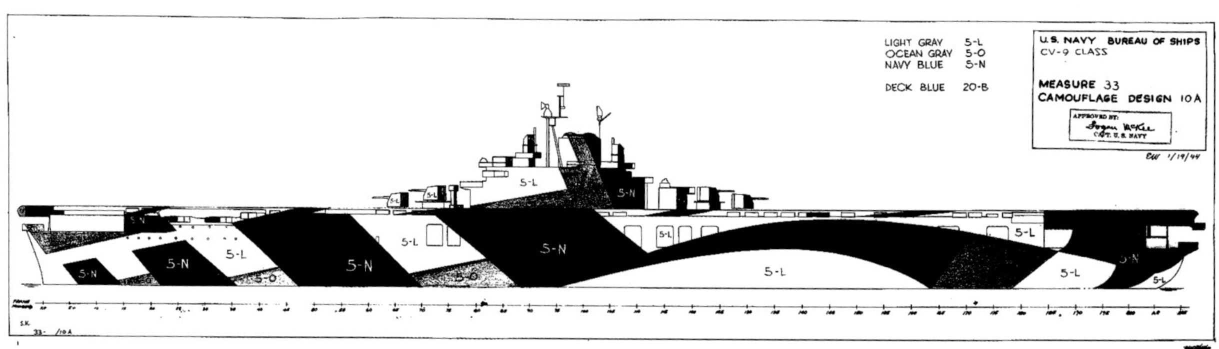

Camouflage

Ship camouflage during World War II used different systems, called measures, and designs based on the type of ship. The dazzle patterns popular during much of the war were intended to confuse the enemy as to a ship's true course and speed and reflected concern for attack by submarines. Later, as the kamikazes became a threat, the Navy reverted to solid color schemes to reduce observation from the air. *Yorktown* was commissioned in Measure 21 with all vertical surfaces painted in Navy Blue (5-N). Sometime prior to May 1944 she was repainted in Measure 33, Design10A, either at Pearl Harbor or Majuro. This pattern used Navy Blue (5-N), Ocean Gray (5-O), and Light Gray (5-L), but Pale Gray (5-P) may have been used in place of the Light Gray. The *Yorktown* retained her camouflage pattern when she was refitted at Puget Sound in September 1944. Design 10A was considered the most graceful of all the carrier camouflage patterns and was carried on four carriers: the *Wasp*, *Yorktown*, *Ticonderoga*, and *Shangri-La*. *Yorktown* was repainted in Measure 21 before the end of the war. (In 1945, with blue pigment in short supply, many ships were painted in Navy Gray (5-N), which had the same reflectance and designation as Navy Blue (5-N).) In

as a Japanese airbase; the carrier strikes would be anticlimactic. Task Force 58 had sortied from Majuro on 13 April under Mitscher's direct command, with three task groups: Clark's Task Group 58.1 with *Hornet*, *Belleau Wood*, *Cowpens*, and *Bataan*; Montgomery's Task Group 58.2 with *Bunker Hill*, *Yorktown*, *Monterey*, and *Cabot*; and Reeves' Task Group 58.3 with *Enterprise*, *Lexington*, *Princeton*, and *Langley*. The task force feinted toward Palau, then hit New Guinea in the Wakde–Sarmi area on 21 April before striking the landing areas on the 22nd and 23rd in direct support of the landing troops. Only snooper aircraft from the west had harassed Clark's task group and the Japanese offered only token resistance, so the operation went smoothly. Mitscher used his night fighters to watch for night torpedo attacks and to keep the Japanese troops awake. On 24 April, the task force withdrew to a new fleet anchorage at Manus in the Admiralties, at the northwestern end of the Bismarck Archipelago. Later landings at Wakde, Biak, Noemfoor, and Sansapor carried MacArthur's forces to the northwestern tip of New Guinea, the Vogelkop (Bird's Head) Peninsula, 550 miles west of Hollandia in a little more than three months.

TRUK AGAIN

Japan had started to rebuild Truk as a bomber base and increased its antiaircraft defenses. When word of the buildup reached Nimitz, he ordered Mitscher to hit Truk again, and Task Force 58 sortied from Manus. The second carrier battle for Truk began with a predawn fighter sweep on 29 April. The immediate Japanese response was a torpedo-plane attack on Task Force 58. *Bunker Hill* reported three groups of unidentified aircraft approaching from the northwest, and fighters were vectored out to intercept. Minutes later the combat air patrol sighted fifteen enemy fighters closing in from the northeast. At 0816 the screen opened fire on three Jill torpedo bombers on *Yorktown*'s starboard bow.

She began evasive maneuvers and opened fire on the lead plane, which crashed in flames and then shifted her fire to the remaining two. One crashed off the port bow, but the other, although hit repeatedly, continued to bore in; it crossed the bow before finally crashing off the port beam, never having released its torpedo. While this was taking place the screen brought down another Jill that crashed 3,000 yards off *Yorktown*'s port quarter.

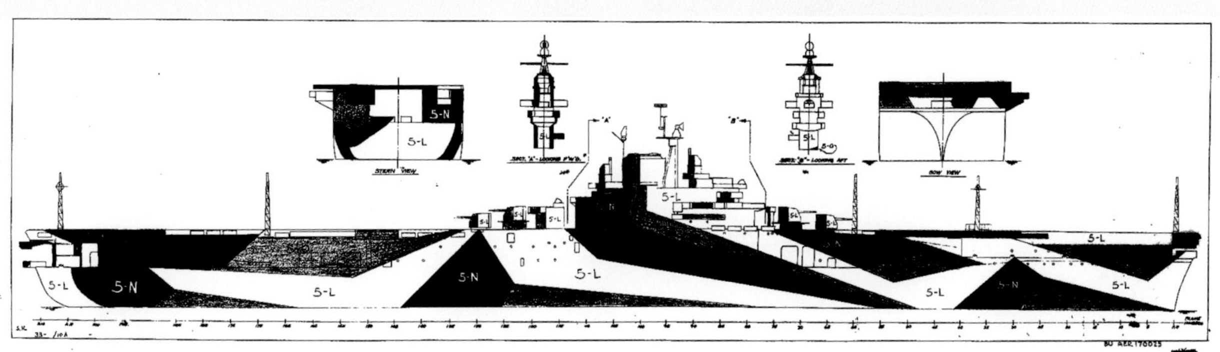

Camouflage Measure 33, Design 10A as applied to *Yorktown* in mid-1944. The colors used were: Light Gray 5-L, Ocean Gray 5-O, Navy Blue 5-N, and Deck Blue 20-B. *Yorktown* would carry this dazzle pattern into 1945. (U.S. Navy)

all the camouflage measures used on aircraft carriers, horizontal surfaces were solid Deck Blue (20-B).

The actual color of the flight deck varied because of weathering and other factors. A darker version of the flight deck stain, matching Deck Blue (20-B), came into use in 1944. *Yorktown*'s crew repainted her flight deck in this darker blue between flight operations in May 1945. Her deck markings varied over time. At her commissioning *Yorktown* had a wide solid white stripe running down the middle of the flight deck and dashed lines on either edge. Later these stripes were painted black. At one point her hull number was painted on the bow and stern in large white numbers, with the bow numbers reading "backwards" since she had arresting gear forward and could recover aircraft by backing down. Later in the war her hull numbers were in black in the "normal" positions on the bow and stern with white dashed lines on the flight deck edges but the dashed line down the middle of the flight deck was slightly off center.

Meanwhile, over Truk antiaircraft fire was intense. Dozens of Zeros challenged the Hellcats, but the quality of Japanese pilots had deteriorated, and by midmorning Task Force 58 controlled the air over Truk. The next day more aircraft were destroyed on the ground. Although the Americans lost aircraft, more than half of their aircrews were picked up, many by the submarine *Tang* alone. At this point, though heavy antiaircraft defenses and a few aircraft remained, the Japanese could no longer maintain Truk as a major airbase. Mitscher detached heavy surface ships for shelling missions elsewhere—cruisers shelled Satawan, 160 miles to the southeast, on 30 April, and Vice Adm. Willis A. "Ching" Lee formed a battle line to shell Ponape, 380 miles west. On 1 May, Clark's Task Group 58.1 provided air cover for the battleships while TGs 58.2 and 58.3 headed for Majuro, reaching it on 4 May. *Yorktown* got under way again two days later, this time for Oahu, arriving at Pearl Harbor on the 11th. For the next eighteen days she conducted training in the Hawaiian Islands for Air Group 1, which was replacing Air Group 5. On 29 May she headed back to the Central Pacific, entering Majuro Lagoon on 3 June to prepare for her next major operation, supporting an amphibious assault on the Marianas.

A Japanese torpedo plane makes a run on *Yorktown* off Truk, 29 April 1944. (NNAM)

Yorktown at Majuro before departing for the Marianas, June 1944. (U.S. Navy)

TO THE MARIANAS

FORAGER: THE OPENING MOVES

Operation Forager, the capture of the Southern Marianas, 3,000 miles west of Pearl Harbor, was carried out to establish bases from which the Army Air Forces' new long-range B-29 bombers could reach Japan. The target date for the invasion of Saipan was 15 June 1944. Guam, the southernmost island in the chain, had been an American possession for nearly 40 years before the war, but Japan considered Saipan home territory. Its loss would be regarded as a breach of Japan's inner lines of defense. For the coming operation *Yorktown* would be under Jocko Clark as part of Task Group 58.1 along with *Hornet*, *Belleau Wood*, and *Bataan*.

On 6 June, Task Force 58 stood out of Majuro and set a course for the Marianas. Five days later the task force reached its launch point east of Guam and began sending strikes to soften up targets before the Saipan landings. *Yorktown* aircrews concentrated primarily on airfields on Guam. Those raids continued until the 13th.

Mitscher knew through intelligence intercepts that the Japanese were staging aircraft through the Bonin and Volcano Islands to the north, principally Iwo Jima and Chichi Jima. He decided to send two task groups there. Clark's Task Group 58.1, with *Yorktown*, and Rear Adm. William K. "Keen" Harrill's TG 58.4 were to launch two days of strikes against the Bonins. When it was learned that the Japanese carrier forces were headed toward the Marianas, Mitscher ordered Clark to limit the strikes to a single day, but Clark, being more aggressive than Harrill, raced north and got in strikes against Iwo Jima and Chichi Jima on the 15th, ahead of worsening weather. On the 16th there was a slight break in the weather just after noon, and Clark launched strikes on Iwo Jima that caught the Japanese completely by surprise. Harrill did not launch, citing low fuel and heavy weather. The two task groups headed back to the Marianas to join what was to be the battle of the Philippine Sea. Task Force 58 reunited on 18 June and awaited the approaching carriers of the Japanese First Mobile Fleet.

In May Adm. Soemu Toyoda, the new commander in chief of the Combined Fleet, had launched Operation A-Go, an attempt to lure Spruance into the waters between the Palaus, Yap, and Woleai, where Japanese land-based and carrier aircraft would annihilate the American fleet in a "decisive battle." The First Mobile Fleet, under Adm. Jisaburo Ozawa, included nine carriers, five battleships, seven heavy cruisers,

Yorktown during operations in the Marianas. Hellcats, Avengers, and Helldivers of Air Group 1 are spotted aft. (U.S. Navy)

thirty-four destroyers, and six oilers. Carrier Division 1 included *Shokaku*, *Zuikaku*, and the new 33,000-ton *Taiho*. Carrier Division 2 had *Hiyo*, *Junyo*, and *Ryuho*, And Carrier Division 3 *Chitose*, *Chiyoda*, and *Zuiho*. Ozawa could muster more than 400 carrier aircraft and was counting on land-based aircraft from island bases in range. He could also enjoy the "weather gauge." He would be steaming into the prevailing easterly wind, which meant he could close with the American fleet while launching, whereas the Americans would have to reverse course to do so. Since the ranges of Japanese carrier aircraft were longer than those of their American counterparts, Ozawa could stay out of range. Finally, his carrier aircraft would be able to land on island bases to refuel and rearm for further attacks.

PHILIPPINE SEA: THE "MARIANAS TURKEY SHOOT"

American search planes did not sight the Japanese on the 18th or on the morning of the 19th. At that point *Lexington*, flagship of Task Force 58, was about 90 miles northwest of Guam and about 100 miles southwest of Saipan. The task force was arrayed in the shape of a giant backward letter *F*. In a line from north to south, twelve nautical miles apart, were Clark's Task Group 58.1 with *Hornet*, *Yorktown*, *Belleau Wood*, and *Bataan*;

A Hellcat from the VF-1 "Top Hatter" F6F-3 launching from *Yorktown* during the "Marianas Turkey Shoot," 19 June 1944. (U.S. Navy)

Reeves' Task Group 58.3 with *Lexington*, *Enterprise*, *Princeton*, and *San Jacinto*; then Montgomery's TG 58.2 with *Bunker Hill*, *Wasp*, *Cabot*, and *Monterey*. Harrill's Task Group 58.4, with *Essex*, *Cowpens*, and *Langley*, was twelve nautical miles west of Clark, and Vice Admiral Lee's Battle Line, Task Group 58.7, with the fast battleships *Washington*, *North Carolina*, *Iowa*, *New Jersey*, *South Dakota*, and *Alabama*, was fifteen nautical miles west of the middle task group, 58.3. Radar picket destroyers were stationed to the west of the battleships.

On the morning of the 19th *Yorktown* aircraft began to strike Japanese airbases on Guam. Clashes with Japanese aircraft based there continued until midmorning, when the first indication of carrier planes closing in from the west appeared on radar. At that point *Yorktown* sent part of her air group back to hit Guam again and another part out to meet the incoming raid; she would continue to do so throughout the battle. That day *Yorktown* aircraft claimed dozens of enemy planes destroyed—her part of the "Marianas Turkey Shoot"—and dropped tons of bombs on the Guam bases.

THE FLIGHT BEYOND DARKNESS

On the 20th, Task Force 58 was about 320 miles from the Japanese fleet and, as Japanese planners had foreseen, downwind of it. But American planners originally estimated the distance to be only about 230 miles, under (but close to) the maximum range for strike aircraft. An immediate launch would mean a night recovery, and only a handful of the pilots had night training. Mitscher nevertheless gave the order to launch, and all twelve carriers in Task Groups 58.1, 58.2, and 58.3 began putting aircraft in the air at 1624. The Japanese carriers were the main targets, but by this time they were still 60 nautical miles farther west than the strike planners had briefed. As it was, all the aircraft flew at "maximum conserve" throttle settings, but it would be touch and go for many of the aircrews when they returned.

That afternoon a *Hornet* pilot spotted the Japanese fleet. *Yorktown* had launched a 40-plane strike between 1623 and 1643. The sun was just touching the horizon as the aircraft arrived over the target.

Planes from *Hornet*, *Yorktown*, and *Bataan* attacked *Zuikaku*, claiming eight hits, and several Hellcats strafed her bridge, but her evasive action kept her clear of two torpedoes and several bombs. The one direct bomb hit on *Zuikaku* landed aft of the island, rupturing the aviation fuel system and starting fires, but damage control by her crew saved her. Several other ships in the Japanese force were attacked, though no confirmed sinkings were credited to the *Yorktown* air group. Lt. Charles Nelson of *Yorktown*'s VT-1 led a torpedo attack against *Ryuho* but was shot down; no one from his

Japanese carriers under attack by Task Force 58, 20 June 1944. (U.S. Navy)

Helldivers and Avengers of Air Group 1. (U.S. Navy)

crew survived. *Ryuho* dodged all five torpedoes from the group. That night the Combined Fleet commander directed the remaining Japanese forces to retire.

The strike aircraft now straggled back toward the carriers in the dark. Damaged aircraft dropped behind, many to be lost. A new moon and overcast further hampered the pilots. Some ran out of fuel before they reached the carriers. Mitscher's staff had planned to light up the task force at the right moment to guide them in, but Clark, apparently unaware of this, ordered Task Group 58.1 to turn on the lights before Mitscher gave the order—"Turn on the lights!"—and the task force lit up, sending searchlight beams and star shells into the overcast sky. "Tell 'em to land on any carrier." *Yorktown* began recoveries at 2043 and continued until 2205. Of the 40 aircraft launched by *Yorktown* only 14 returned. Thirteen landed on other carriers and *Yorktown* recovered 14 from other carriers. Two Avengers and their crews were lost to enemy action.

On 21 June, TF 58 attempted to catch the remaining enemy ships but gave up that evening when air searches failed to gain contact with them. Most of the task force retired to Eniwetok, now a rear area, but *Yorktown* returned to the Marianas with Task Group 58.1 for air strikes on Pagan, in the Northern Marianas, on the 22nd and 23rd.

(above) Burning fuel dumps and small trawlers set afire by low-flying Hellcats off Haha Jima Island, 4 July 1944. (U.S. Navy)

(left) SB2C-1C Helldivers approach *Yorktown* for landing, July 1944. (U.S. Navy)

(below) Task Force 58 strikes Orote Airfield, Guam, as seen from a VT-1 Avenger, 7 July 1944. Smoke marks destroyed antiaircraft batteries. (U.S. Navy)

A Hellcat lands on *Yorktown* without a tailhook during strikes on the Bonins, 24 July 1944. Deck crew members duck as the tires smoke under the strain of full braking. (U.S. Navy)

On the 24th, Clark was given permission to hit the Bonins again, and the task group aircraft took off in heavy seas to strike "the Jimas."

The Japanese sent three strikes against the task group, all of which were intercepted and ultimately repulsed. The last two strikes managed to reach the task group, but antiaircraft fire helped drive them off. The Japanese lost dozens of aircraft and, for the time being, were no longer able to attack the Americans off Saipan and Guam. Task Group 58.1 reached Eniwetok on the 27th, the last of the three task groups.

On 30 June, Clark's Task Group 58.1 and TG 58.2, now under Rear Adm. Ralph E. "Dave" Davison, were sent to hit the Bonins again, which they did on the 3rd and 4th of July.

On the way back south, both task groups hit Guam and Rota in rotation for a week.

On 23 July, *Yorktown* headed west for a series of raids on Yap, Ulithi, and the Palaus. She carried out those attacks on 25 July and arrived back in the Marianas on the 29th.

She would miss the battles at Leyte Gulf of 23 to 26 October, which by some criteria would be regarded collectively as the largest naval battle in history, but *Yorktown* would play her part in the final critical battles of the war.

THE PHILIPPINES

OVERHAUL

On 31 July 1944 *Yorktown* left the Marianas and headed for Eniwetok, then to Pearl Harbor, and then to the West Coast. *Yorktown* arrived at the Puget Sound Navy Yard, Bremerton, Washington, on 17 August to begin a two-month overhaul. Capt. Thomas S. Combs took command of *Yorktown* from Captain Jennings on 29 September. Combs would take *Yorktown*, with many new and inexperienced crew members and a new air group, Air Group 3, back into the most intense combat of the war. His leadership would keep up the morale of the aircrews despite the rough weather in which the carriers often operated. On 6 October her overhaul was completed; on the 9th *Yorktown* departed Puget Sound and from the 11th to the 13th loaded planes and supplies at the Alameda Naval Air Station before heading back to the western Pacific. She stopped at Pearl Harbor from the 18th to the 24th to bring Air Group 3 on board. *Yorktown* arrived back at Eniwetok on 31 October, departed the next day, and on the 3rd reached Ulithi, now a U.S. fleet anchorage, to become part of Task Group 38.4, with which she got under way on 5 November. Halsey had replaced Spruance, and under the "two platoon" system of command in the Pacific the Fifth Fleet had become the Third Fleet. Task Force 58, the fast carriers, became Task Force 38.

Overhaul

Yorktown had five radio masts when commissioned; three were removed during her overhaul in Bremerton, leaving only the forward pair. The number of 40-mm mounts on the island shrank to three when the flag bridge was expanded, but several quad 40-mm mounts elsewhere were added or improved upon: two were added on the port-side sponson at the hangar-deck level when the hangar-deck catapult was removed and a second flight-deck catapult added; two went on a remodeled and enlarged stern sponson; three mounts were added on the starboard side on sponsons just below the island; the two aft on the starboard quarter at the hangar deck were "sponsoned out" to give them better fields of fire; and two mounts aft on the port side on the gallery deck were added. This gave *Yorktown* a total of seventeen 40-mm quad mounts. The number of 20-mm mounts increased as well. Also, it was now that CIC was moved to larger spaces on the gallery deck.

LEYTE

The hectic pace of operations during the Leyte operation had left Task Force 38 at the end of its endurance. By the end of October, the fast carriers were almost out of ammunition and food, for which, unlike fuel, replenishment techniques had not yet been developed at this point in the war. Continuing Japanese air raids caused MacArthur to request that both the fast carriers and the escort carriers stay on a while longer, and the fast carriers did, covering Leyte and attacking targets in the Philippines. Pilot fatigue had become chronic—so much so that when Halsey rotated Vice Adm. John S. McCain Sr.'s Task Group 38.1 and Sherman's TG 38.3 to Ulithi for replacement air groups, two of the outgoing groups had served only five of the required six months in a combat zone. The kamikazes, which had made their debut during the battles off Leyte Gulf, were a continuing threat. *Intrepid* had taken a hit on 29 October, *Franklin* and *Belleau Wood* on the 30th. While at Ulithi, Mitscher turned command of Task Force 38 over to Vice Admiral McCain, who had been in a "learning status" as commander of Task Group 38.1, where Montgomery relieved him.

Yorktown left Ulithi on 5 November with Task Group 38.4 but two days later was shifted to 38.1, and Montgomery shifted his flag to her from *Hornet* on the 9th. For the next two weeks, *Yorktown* launched air strikes on shore targets.

On the 11th the task group headed to a launch point northeast of Leyte from which it struck a Japanese convoy being escorted to Ormoc Bay on the west coast.

Yorktown launched her first strike against the convoy that morning and sent another later in the day. Air Group 3 claimed two destroyers sunk, one probably sunk, and another damaged. A Hellcat was shot down by flak near the convoy, but the pilot made a successful water landing, was rescued by a native outrigger and taken to Samar, where he was later picked up. Although there were several radar contacts throughout the day, no interceptions were made. The next day *Yorktown* headed for a dawn refueling rendezvous and put up CAP and ASW cover during the day. On the 13th the task group headed for a launch point a hundred miles off Baker Bay on Luzon from which to strike airfields, shipping, fleet units, and harbor installations on central and southern Luzon. Air Group 3 made three strikes against shipping in Manila Bay and the Mindoro Strait and sent a fighter sweep over the airfield at Legazpi. A Hellcat in the latter was hit by flak and lost. Another Hellcat failed to join up on the return flight; also, a Helldiver damaged by flak made a water landing near a picket destroyer, which picked up the crew. CAP and ASW patrols were also flown throughout the day, *Yorktown*'s CAP claiming two shootdowns. The strikes against shipping were repeated the next day, and two more Hellcats were lost. Task Group 58.1 then withdrew to the southeast for another refueling rendezvous and to take replacement aircraft on board.

The slender air defenses over U.S. forces in Leyte Gulf had led to a Japanese counterattack, which caused American commanders to send Sherman's Task Group 38.3 back to join Rear Adm. Gerald F. Bogan's TG 38.2 in protecting shipping off Leyte. Strikes against airfields and installations on Luzon by Montgomery's Task Group 38.1 and Bogan's Task Group 38.2 on 19 November marked the end of fast carrier operations in support of the Leyte campaign. On that day two Hellcats were lost to flak over Mabalacat and another made a water landing near a destroyer, which picked up the pilot. Bombing aircraft destroyed several enemy planes and ships, including a heavy cruiser, but the kamikazes had struck back, hitting *Intrepid*, *Essex*, and *Cabot* and damaging the *Hancock* with a near miss.

Following the strikes of the 19th, Task Group 38.1 retired at high speed to the east. *Yorktown* detached on the 23rd and arrived the next day at Ulithi, where she remained until 10 December. She rejoined Task Force 38 on the 13th to strike airfields on Luzon from the 14th to the 16th to eliminate Japanese aircraft that might interfere with the landings on the west coast of Mindoro on 15 December. She maintained continuous coverage throughout the day and sent night fighters over Luzon on "heckler" missions. Each night the task group would withdraw to the east at high speed and the next day repeat the process. Although little air opposition was met, antiaircraft fire was especially heavy over Nichols and Nielson airfields, just south of Manila; several Hellcats were hit and returned with damage. Two strafing Hellcats failed to return on the

Countering the Kamikazes

The damage being done by the kamikazes led Halsey to insist that the fast carriers not be exposed to further attacks until better defenses could be devised. McCain, with his operations officer Cdr. John S. "Jimmy" Thach and the rest of the fast carrier staff, developed defensive tactics that best utilized the increasing number of fighters assigned to carrier air groups. At the advice of Jocko Clark, McCain enlarged the task group cruising formations horizontally, by stationing radar picket ships, called "Tomcats," sixty miles ahead of the carriers. McCain also started several new combat air patrols: JACKCAP, two to four fighters flying at low altitude in each of the four quadrants; DADCAP, patrols at all altitudes launched at dawn and relieved at dusk by BATCAP night fighters; RAPCAP radar picket planes; and SCOCAP, a scouting line of planes stationed over the Tomcat radar picket destroyers. Returning air strikes would circle over the Tomcats to be "deloused": any aircraft not making the specified identifying turn would be picked off by the defending fighters. Commander Thach also developed the "Three Strike" system, whereby one fighter patrol would remain over an enemy airfield while a second prepared to take off and a third was either on its way to or from the target or was being readied for another strike. The constant patrolling would be continued at night by "heckling" night fighters flying over enemy airfields to discourage night attacks. These measures were part of what McCain called his "Big Blue Blanket" for protecting the carrier task force. All these techniques were practiced in simulated "Moosetrap" training strikes during maneuvers off Ulithi in late November and early December 1944.

first day. One was seen to crash at Nichols, but the other made a water landing near a destroyer, which recovered the pilot. On the 15th two more damaged Hellcats made water landings, and again the pilots were picked up. On the 16th, Cdr. Macpherson B. "Mac" Williams, skipper of Air Group 3, was shot down five miles west of Marakin Airfield to the east of Manila and was seen to bail out of his Hellcat; Filipino guerilla forces eventually spirited Mac Williams, along with two other *Yorktown* pilots, to safety. At the end of the three days of strikes Task Force 38 had destroyed about 200 Japanese planes on and over Luzon. Worsening weather covered the task force as it withdrew to the east to refuel.

HALSEY'S TYPHOON

On the 17th, as the task force began its retirement from the Luzon strikes, the weather began to worsen.

***Yorktown*'s crew on the hangar deck watch the fleet premiere of the movie *The Fighting Lady*, Ulithi, 5 February 1945.**

The Fighting Lady

The Fighting Lady was a 1944 documentary film directed by the famous photographer Edward Steichen, who served as a reserve commander documenting the Navy's war, and William Wyler, who was not credited. It was produced by the Navy and narrated by actor Robert Taylor, who was also a naval aviator, a reserve lieutenant. It depicted life aboard an anonymous aircraft carrier, later identified as *Yorktown*, although some scenes were shot on board her sister ship *Ticonderoga*. Real officers were featured, including Admiral Mitscher, Admiral McCain, Captain Clark (referred to in the film as "Jocko" and voiced by Harry Morgan), and Capt. Dixie Kiefer, commanding *Ticonderoga* (and referred to as "Dixie"). Spectacular color photography, including gun-camera footage from assaults on Marcus, Kwajalein, Truk, and Tinian Islands, and culminating with the battle of the Philippine Sea, made for a powerful visual impact. The film was awarded an Oscar in 1945 for best documentary.

While at Ulithi on 5 February, the fleet premiere of the movie *The Fighting Lady* took place aboard *Yorktown* and the evening included a buffet supper. An original print of the film was presented to the ship by the producer, Lt. Cdr. Dwight Long, a member of Steichen's Naval Aviation Photographic Unit. As the film was shown for the crew on the hangar deck there were cheers at the stirring action, friendly catcalls as familiar faces flashed on the screen, and breathless attention when tense moments were relived as a Japanese aircraft kept boring in. One crewman later recalled, "I thought that so-and-so never was going to stop" and that he breathed a sigh of relief when the attacker was brought down. The documentary would not be the only time *Yorktown* appeared in films. Scenes shot on board were also used in the 1944 action drama *Wing and a Prayer*, starring Don Ameche, Dana Andrews, and Charles Bickford.

Halsey did not consider it to be a typhoon until noon the next day, when he finally canceled a refueling then being attempted and strikes planned for Luzon. The task force headed south into a storm blowing east to west. Planes on the light carriers broke their lashings and careened around, starting fires on the *Monterey* and *Cowpens*. Others were lost overboard as carriers plunged wildly into the mountainous waves. Destroyers, low on fuel and without enough ballast to keep them steady, had the worst time of it. Three of them, *Spence*, *Hull*, and *Monaghan*, capsized and sank with the loss of nearly all hands. *Yorktown* took part in the rescue operations for the survivors until the 23rd and was back at Ulithi the next day.

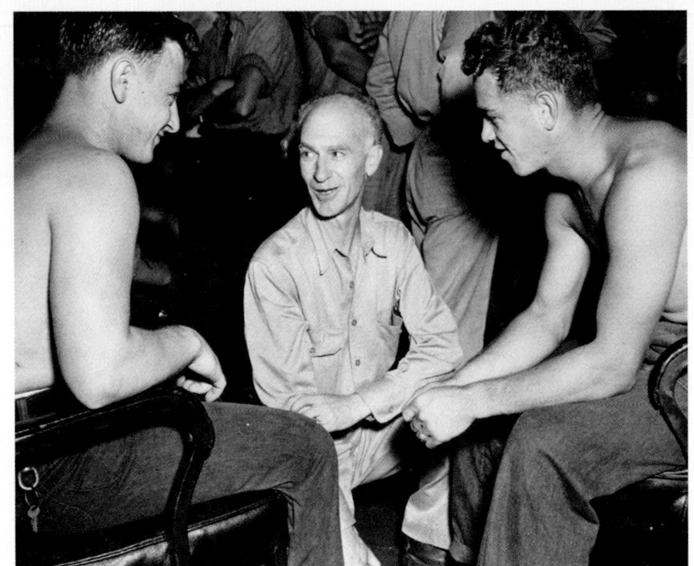

Ernie Pyle talks with *Yorktown* sailors while the ship was anchored at Ulithi, 5 February 1945. (U.S. Navy)

Ernie Pyle

The Pulitzer Prize–winning journalist and war correspondent Ernie Pyle was best known for his stories about ordinary American soldiers. He had reported on the Battle of Britain from London in 1940 and from late 1942 covered combat in North Africa, Italy, and Normandy before returning to the United States in September 1944, suffering from combat stress. He reluctantly agreed to cover the Pacific in January 1945 and spent time with various Navy and Marine units and was on board *Yorktown* in February 1945 while she was at Ulithi. During the battle of Okinawa he was killed by enemy fire on Ie Shima, a nearby island being seized for its airfields.

INTO THE SOUTH CHINA SEA

Yorktown put out to sea on 30 December with Task Force 38 for strikes on Luzon and Formosa (Taiwan) airfields to support the Lingayen Gulf landings scheduled for 3 January 1945. *Yorktown* hit targets on Formosa on the 3rd and 4th, rendezvoused for fueling on the 5th, and sent her planes against Luzon targets and shipping on the 6th and 7th. The 8th brought another fueling rendezvous, and on the 9th she conducted her last attack on Formosa; the Japanese sent heavy air attacks against the forces bound for Lingayen Gulf, and McCain shifted his strikes from Formosa to the Luzon area.

On 10 January, Task Force 38 entered the South China Sea via the Bashi Channel to begin a series of raids on Japan's inner defenses. Halsey had wanted to track down the surviving Japanese surface units from the Leyte Gulf battles—the "hermaphrodite" battleships (backfitted with flying-off decks aft) *Ise* and *Hyuga*—in Indochina, but they were gone by the time Task Force 38's strikes arrived in the area of Saigon and Tourane Bay on 12 January. Its aviators still managed to sink dozens of enemy ships, including several warships. *Yorktown* fueled on the 13th and on the 15th launched raids on Formosa and Canton (Guangzhou). The next day she hit Hong Kong and, again, Canton. Heavy weather made refueling difficult on the 17th, 18th, and 19th, but Halsey ran north for a series of strikes against Formosa and nearby portions of the Chinese coast on 15 January. Hong Kong, Hainan, Canton, Swatow, and Macao were hit the next day, with minimal results. On 20 January *Yorktown* exited the South China Sea with Task Force 38 via the Balintang Channel. She participated in a raid on Formosa on the 21st and another on Okinawa on the 22d before clearing the area with Task Force 38 for Ulithi, which she entered the morning of 26 January. On the same day Spruance replaced Halsey, and accordingly the Third Fleet again became the Fifth Fleet and Task Force 38, Task Force 58. Mitscher would again command the fast carriers, for the next phase of the Pacific War.

IWO JIMA AND OKINAWA

Before the final assault on Japan could take place, the seizure of islands within the strategic triangle formed by Formosa, Saipan, and Tokyo had to be considered. Spruance had recommended taking Okinawa in the Ryukyus Islands and now suggested seizing Iwo Jima in the Bonins for an airbase. Spruance added, however, that a method of transferring ammunition at sea would be needed for these assaults, because of the distances from friendly bases. Until this time, fuel had been transferred at sea but ammunition only from lighters in protected anchorages. Mitscher's Task Force 58 included: Clark's Task Group 58.1; Dave Davison's TG 58.2; Ted Sherman's TG 58.3; and Arthur Radford's Task 58.4. Matt Gardner led the night carrier group, Task Group 58.5.

IWO JIMA

The eastern leg of the strategic triangle, Saipan to Tokyo, was the route flown by B-29s on their way to targets in Japan. A halfway point was needed both to recover damaged B-29s unable to make it back to the Marianas and as a base for fighter escorts. Only Iwo Jima met these requirements. The original date for the landings was set at 20 January 1945, but prolonged resistance on Leyte and Luzon pushed the target date back to 19 February. *Yorktown* had remained at Ulithi arming, provisioning, and conducting upkeep until 10 February, when she sortied with Radford on board as commander of Task Group 58.4 for a series of raids on Japanese islands to support the landings on Iwo Jima.

Four Hellcats over Iwo Jima in support of Marines, 21 February 1945, from a *Yorktown* plane. (U.S. Navy)

Yorktown Helldivers en route to bombing targets on Iwo Jima, 22 February 1945. (U.S. Navy)

Spruance and Mitscher both flew their flags in Task Group 58.3, Spruance on board the cruiser *Indianapolis* and Mitscher in *Bunker Hill*. At 0642 on the 16th *Yorktown* began launching the first of seven strikes against aircraft, installations, and shipping in and around Tokyo, while the light carriers *Langley* and *Cabot* maintained the CAP over the task group throughout the day. The air opposition over Tokyo was not very impressive; the Japanese had apparently been taken by surprise. One Hellcat, damaged during an encounter with a group of Nates, made a water landing next to a picket destroyer, which rescued the pilot. The strikes were repeated the next day.

That evening Task Force 58 headed south to refuel and to support the landings on Iwo Jima. On the 18th Air Group 3 hit Chichi Jima in the Bonins. On the 20th *Yorktown* launched three support strikes—Hellcats, Helldivers, and Avengers loaded with bombs, rockets, and napalm—as well as two fighter sweeps, over Iwo Jima and Chichi Jima, respectively.

No air opposition was encountered, and all planes returned to the ship. The air around Iwo Jima continued to attract kamikazes, however. On the 21st the old *Saratoga* (CV-3), which had joined the escort carriers off Iwo to provide night cover, was hit by (but survived) four bombs and two kamikazes, and the escort carrier *Bismarck Sea* was lost to a lone kamikaze.

Yorktown returned for strikes in the Tokyo area on the 25th, sending two raids to bomb and strife airfields. On the 26th, her aircraft made a sweep of installations on Kyushu before she retired with Task Group 58.4 to Ulithi, entering the anchorage on 1 March. On the 6th, Air Group 9 replaced Group 3 at Ulithi to operate from *Yorktown* during the coming operations. While at Ulithi ships darkened at night, but on the 11th a long-range, twin-engined Frances kamikaze flew all the way to Ulithi and crashed into the after flight deck of the new *Randolph*, which was lighted while loading ammunition. *Yorktown* departed Ulithi on the 14th.

OKINAWA

The fast carriers resumed raids on Japan in support of the Okinawa landings scheduled for 1 April. Task Force 57, the British carrier force, was positioned to

Kamikaze (right) hit during attack on *Langley* and *Yorktown* about to crash, 18 March 1945. (U.S. Navy)

the southwest, between Okinawa and Formosa, while Task Force 58 was between Okinawa and Kyushu. On 18 March, *Yorktown* arrived off Japan and began launching strikes on airfields on Kyushu, Honshu, and Shikoku. Her task group soon came under air attack.

The action started at 0739, when a Judy dropped a bomb on the deck of *Enterprise* from such a low altitude that it bounced. The detonator separated from the bomb and exploded itself against the island, causing minor damage; the bomb stopped on the deck and did not explode. At 0800, a twin-engine Frances attacked *Yorktown* from her port quarter. *Yorktown* opened fire and began scoring hits. The plane began to burn but continued its run, passing over the bow and splashing in the water off to starboard. Seven minutes later another Frances attacked, but it too was shot down by the combined fire of the formation and crashed close aboard *Intrepid*'s starboard side. No other attacks developed until that afternoon, when three Judy dive-bombers attacked. At 1309 a Judy dove on *Yorktown* from the starboard bow and dropped a bomb that landed close aboard to port alongside the elevator. The Judy was already on fire before dropping its bomb and crashed off the port beam. At 1317 another Judy came in off the starboard bow at low altitude and dropped a bomb that landed close aboard to starboard. Its explosion did no structural damage but knocked the gyros out of commission for a while.

This Judy too had been afire before dropping its bomb and crashed astern. The third Judy dove on

Yorktown hit during "Bomb Sunday," 18 March 1945. (Yorktown Association)

Yorktown at 1500, coming out of the clouds dead ahead and obtaining a hit.

It too had been taken under fire by the ship's guns and had begun to disintegrate before reaching her. When it pulled out of its dive it broke in two, and the crew bailed out. (One was picked up by a destroyer.) The bomb hit the starboard wing of the signal bridge and passed through to the second deck before exploding. It punched two large holes through the side and caused minor damage to nearby spaces.

Damage to the interior of the island. (Yorktown Association)

An officer and four enlisted crewmen were killed on the second deck and another twenty-six wounded. One of the wounded was permanently blinded, and another had to have a five-pound fragment of the bomb removed from his abdomen. This was the only time *Yorktown* was hit during the war, and because it was the week before Palm Sunday her crew remembered it afterward as "Bomb Sunday." (In the midst of these attacks Air Group 9's ace Gene Valencia was trying to recover with a jammed tailhook. He made four passes but got waved off each time, because his tailhook did not budge. He eventually had to make a water landing and was picked up by a destroyer.) The bogies were prevalent during the rest of the afternoon and into the night but no more ships in the task group were damaged.

The next day Davison's Task Group 58.2 was hit hard. *Wasp* was hit by an undetected aircraft and suffered heavy casualties. While *Franklin*, Davison's flagship, was launching a strike, a lone Japanese aircraft dropped two bombs on her flight deck, causing massive fires and explosions. *Franklin* became the most heavily damaged aircraft carrier to survive the war. Japanese aircraft had also closed in on the *Enterprise*, their bombs missing but friendly antiaircraft fire causing a flight-deck fire. *Yorktown* continued air operations against the three southernmost Japanese islands before retiring for fueling operations on the 20th. On the 22nd Task Force 58 replenished and was reorganized into three task groups, leaving Davison's 58.2 as a "cripple" task group—that is to escort the damaged *Franklin*, *Enterprise*, and *Wasp* back to Ulithi. Clark's TG 58.1 now included *Hornet*, *Belleau Wood*, *San Jacinto*, and *Bennington*. Sherman's TG 58.3 included *Essex*, *Bunker Hill*, *Hancock*, *Bataan*, and *Cabot*, while Radford's Task Group 58.4 had *Yorktown*, *Intrepid*, *Langley*, and the newly arrived *Independence*. Strikes to soften up Okinawa were conducted from the 23d through the 28th of March before heading back to Japanese waters for an additional strike on the Home Islands. On the 29th *Yorktown* put two raids and one photo reconnaissance mission over Kyushu. Around 1410 that afternoon, a single Judy attempted a suicide dive on *Yorktown*. The carrier's antiaircraft gunners opened up and scored numerous hits before the Judy passed over the ship, very near the island, and splashed about 60 feet off the port side. Beginning on 30 March and into the next day, the fast carriers of her task group concentrated on Okinawa and the surrounding islands.

On 1 April as the assault troops stormed ashore *Yorktown* sent her planes to support the troops directly. For nearly six weeks she continued this support, retiring to the east every three days to rendezvous for refueling and reprovisioning. She also attacked the nearby islands in the Sakishima Gunto from 4 to 6 April. The Japanese had planned to launch from there the first of their *kikusui* (floating chrysanthemum) mass kamikaze attacks to destroy the American fleet when the landings took place, but the prelanding carrier strikes had delayed this major Japanese counterstroke until 7 April. The outer radar picket destroyers were the first to suffer (although a limited number of small-scale air attacks, including kamikazes, and suicide-boat attacks had been made against ships off Okinawa before then). Anticipating further kamikaze attacks Mitscher had ordered that all bomber and torpedo aircraft on board the task force carriers be struck below to the hangar decks and defueled.

DEATH OF *YAMATO*

At the same time they launched the kikusui attacks, the Japanese sent the remainder of their once proud surface fleet on a suicide mission of its own. The superbattleship *Yamato*, the cruiser *Yahagi*, and seven destroyers were to proceed at top speed to Okinawa. It was hoped that *Yamato*, which had only enough fuel for a one-way trip, could beach herself and sink a great many American ships with her 18.1-inch guns before being destroyed. The force left Kure on 6 April but was spotted by the submarines *Threadfin* and *Hackleback* that evening. Alerted by the submarine contact reports, Mitscher prepared to deal with this new threat, ordering the task force north. A search plane from *Essex* discovered the Japanese force just southwest of Kyushu at 0830 on the 7th. Mitscher sent out a strike of 386 aircraft to destroy the Japanese warships. The strikes from the carriers of Task Group 58.4—*Yorktown*, *Intrepid*, *Independence*, and *Langley*—were the last to reach them, and when Air Group 9 aviators arrived *Yamato* was already listing to port, leaking oil and making only ten to fifteen knots; *Yahagi* was dead in the water but with no large fires; and a destroyer was burning and leaking oil but under way. The ships were scattered but clustered into two groups. *Yamato*, screened by four destroyers, was closest. Five miles to the northwest was the hulk of a destroyer, and another five miles beyond, was *Yahagi* with a destroyer alongside.

Yorktown's fliers went after *Yahagi* while *Intrepid* went after *Yamato*. *Intrepid*'s strike leader radioed Lt. Cdr. Herb Houck, leading the *Yorktown* strike, to split his force and send some torpedo bombers against *Yamato*.

Six Avengers accordingly broke away to attack *Yamato*'s exposed starboard side, scoring five torpedo hits on *Yamato* just before the battleship exploded and sank, while the rest of the strike went after *Yahagi*.

The Flying Circus in a publicity photograph probably taken near the end of their tour. Left to right: Lt. Harris Mitchell, Lt. (jg) Clinton Smith, Lt. (jg) James French, and Lt. Eugene Valencia. (U.S. Navy)

Valencia

One of Hellcat divisions of VF-9 was led by Lieutenant Eugene A. Valencia Jr. The division was known as the "Flying Circus." Gene Valencia had become an ace while flying from the *Essex* during Air Group 9's first deployment. His score of seven kills at the time included three at Rabaul, one at Tarawa, and three on the first Truk raid. While preparing for the squadron's next deployment he selected three junior grade lieutenants—Harris Mitchell, Clinton Smith, and James French—for his division and trained them in his "mowing machine" tactics. The Flying Circus became the most successful fighter division of the war and its members all became aces—James French with 11, Harris Mitchell with 10, and Clinton Smith with six. Gene Valencia finished the war with 23 victories, half of them while serving aboard *Yorktown*, and remains the Navy's third-ranking ace of all time.

Hellcats went in ahead, strafing to suppress the antiaircraft fire being thrown up. Hellcats carrying bombs scored two hits, followed by the Helldivers that scored more hits, and Avengers carrying torpedoes. The *Yahagi* rolled on her side and went down. *Yorktown*'s fliers also claimed a destroyer probably sunk and another damaged. For the loss of 10 aircraft and 12 men, the aviators of Task Force 58 sank *Yamato*, *Yahagi*,

Wracked by repeated torpedo hits and explosions, the light cruiser *Yahagi* sinks southwest of Kyushu, 7 April 1945. Photographed by a *Yorktown* plane. (U.S. Navy)

and four destroyers (two of which were sunk and two scuttled), and one of the surviving destroyers had to steam stern first to Japan.

At the conclusion of the action, *Yorktown*'s planes returned to supporting the troops ashore while the fast carriers operated east of Okinawa. On the 9th, Capt. Walter F. Boone was flown on board *Yorktown* by an Avenger from *Enterprise* as her prospective commanding officer. He relieved Captain Combs on 23 April and would remain in command of *Yorktown* through the end of the war. *Yorktown* came under air attack again on the 11th by a single-engine plane. *Yorktown*'s antiaircraft gunners splashed it just inside 2,000 yards.

While off Okinawa, news arrived that the Commander in Chief, President Roosevelt, had died on 12 April. On first hearing of his death, many troops ashore thought it might be a Japanese propaganda trick, but they soon learned it was not. No one had much time to mourn, since Japanese attacks continued unabated.

On the 16th the task group was subjected to two attacks. The first was by five single-engine planes in the early afternoon. One dropped a bomb after diving on the formation and crashed after being hit by gunfire from the ships. Another was also brought down by gunfire and crashed astern of the battleship *Missouri*. A third crashed near a destroyer. The fourth and fifth came in together and headed for *Intrepid*. One was a near miss, but the other crashed on her flight deck, causing extensive damage. The unlucky *Intrepid* was the only ship hit.

The second attack came a few hours later by three single engine planes. Two dove on *Intrepid* and dropped bombs that were near misses. One was shot down by *Intrepid* while the other passed astern of *Yorktown* and was shot down by her gunners. The third was fired on but escaped without dropping a bomb.

On the morning of 17 April Gene Valencia's division of aircraft was assigned to patrol north of the task group formation at 20,000 feet while another division was below it at 18,000 feet. Radar had picked up many contacts closing in, and Valencia ordered the two-aircraft sections flown by Clinton Smith and James

French to engage the dozen or so Japanese aircraft they had encountered while Valencia and Harris Mitchell flew top cover for them. When Smith and French completed their attacks their two sections traded off in the "mowing machine" tactics that the division had practiced before deploying on board *Yorktown*. These tactics were repeated until the surviving kamikazes—all bomb-carrying Zeros, Franks, and Oscars—split up into three-plane formations as they neared the task group. Valencia told his division to pick targets of opportunity as the other *Yorktown* division joined in the fight. As the surviving Japanese turned away, the division, low on fuel, recovered on board *Yorktown*, while other kamikazes were brought down by Hellcats over the picket destroyers and by ships' gunfire. Valencia had achieved "ace in a day" status with six kills and a probable, while Mitchell had three, French four, and Smith one and a probable.

For the rest of April *Yorktown* continued providing air support for the friendly forces on Okinawa. On 1 May, on an otherwise quiet day, three Marine Corsairs from Kadena became lost and were running low on fuel when they were vectored out to the task group. None of the Marine pilots had ever landed on an aircraft carrier before. The first cut his throttle before the landing signal officer (LSO) gave the signal and caught the third wire. The second was high but didn't take the waveoff, landing hard and damaging his tailwheel. The third obeyed all the LSO's signals and made a good landing.

Sporadic air attacks continued until 11 May. *Bunker Hill*, Mitscher's flagship, was east of Okinawa when a Zero headed for her flight deck, dropping a bomb and then crashing into parked aircraft. About the same time, a second kamikaze in a vertical dive smashed into the flight deck near the island, starting an inferno. She was out of the war. Only the *Franklin* had suffered more.

Despite heavy commitments, Mitscher rotated his task groups into Ulithi for rest. Task Group 58.4 detached when TG 58.1 returned on 12 May, and when TG 58.4 returned at the end of May TG 58.3 left for the new base at Leyte. *Yorktown* headed for Ulithi for rest and upkeep with Task Group 58.4, having sustained no additional damage and claiming only one further kill by her antiaircraft battery. While she was at Ulithi, the kamikazes continued to take their toll on the fast carriers. On 14 May a kamikaze found *Enterprise* and hit her, destroying her forward elevator. She would not be repaired before the end of the war. *Yorktown* headed for Okinawa again with Task Group 58.4 on the 24th. On 27 May Halsey relieved Spruance, and the Fifth Fleet again became the Third Fleet. The next day McCain relieved Mitscher as commander of the fast carriers.

Yamato under way but listing to port as *Yorktown* torpedo bombers close in. (NHHC)

Yamato explodes, 7 April 1945. Photographed by a *Yorktown* aircraft. (NHHC)

As seen from *Yorktown*, two Japanese suicide planes attack *Intrepid*, exploding in flames on deck. (U.S. Navy)

FINAL OPERATIONS

On 28 May 1945, the same day McCain relieved Mitscher, *Yorktown* resumed air-support missions over Okinawa; at sea, the kamikazes continued their attacks, taking a heavy toll on the picket destroyers. At the beginning of June *Yorktown* moved northward with Task Force 38 to resume strikes on the Japanese home islands. *Yorktown* was Radford's flagship for TG 38.4, which also comprised *Shangri-La*, *Ticonderoga*, and the light carrier *Independence*. McCain was on board *Shangri-La*, and Halsey was in the battleship *Missouri*. (Halsey had detached Sherman's Task Group 38.3 for a rest period but for his own part joined the other three task groups to hit Japan.) On 2 June the task force launched a special long-range fighter sweep against airfields on southern Kyushu, but bad weather prevented *Yorktown* from hitting two of the three airfields assigned to her. One Hellcat was brought down by antiaircraft fire, and the pilot ditched in Kagoshima Bay. (Although unhurt he was close to the shore, and there were tense moments until he could be picked up by a PBM Mariner "Dumbo" flying boat within range of shore batteries.) On the 3rd *Yorktown* flew four sweeps of airfields and on the 4th returned to Okinawa for support missions.

Halsey's bad luck with weather plagued him again, as Task Force 38 now encountered yet another typhoon. The storm was discovered on the morning of 3 June. By the early evening of the 4th it was heading north, and the task force was heading eastward, away from it. But Halsey on the 5th, not considering the effects on all his task groups, turned the task force westward to cross in front of and ahead of the storm. This course change did not seriously affect Task Group 38.4, with Halsey's and McCain's flagships, but in Clark's TG 38.1 the bow of the cruiser *Pittsburgh* was broken off and the flight-deck bow overhangs on *Hornet* and *Bennington* collapsed. On the 6th and 7th, *Yorktown* resumed Okinawa attacks, also sending strikes back to the Kyushu airfields. On the 9th she launched two days of raids on Minami Daito Shima, southeast of Okinawa. After the second day *Yorktown* retired with TG 38.4 toward Leyte's San Pedro Bay, arriving on 13 June for rest, replenishment, and upkeep.

Air Group 88 replaced Air Group 9 at this point and would serve on board *Yorktown* for the rest of the war. Its fighter-bomber squadron, VBF-88, was equipped with the FG-1D, the version of the Corsair built by Goodyear. *Yorktown* remained at Leyte until 1 July,

Yorktown **at anchor in her final configuration in 1945. (NARA)**

FG-1D Corsair of VBF-88 on board *Yorktown*, 18 July 1945. (NARA)

when Task Group 38.4 got under way to join the rest of the fast carriers in the final series of raids on the Japanese home islands. This time *Bon Homme Richard* replaced *Ticonderoga* and *Cowpens* joined. By 10 July *Yorktown* was off the coast of Japan launching strikes against airfields in the Tokyo area. Air opposition was practically nonexistent; antiaircraft fire was intense but generally inaccurate, although one Hellcat was lost. After a fueling rendezvous on the 11th and 12th the ship resumed strikes on Japan, hitting southern Hokkaido airfields, installations, and shipping on the 14th. VF-88 lost its skipper, Lt. Cdr. Dick Crommelin, that day when his Hellcat collided with another Hellcat in bad weather. On the 15th the weather improved, but a fueling retirement and more heavy weather halted air operations until the 18th, when Air Group 88 returned to the Tokyo area to hit airfields and shipping.

Yorktown fueled and replenished under way from the 19th to the 22nd before resuming air attacks on Japan. Air Group 88 attacked the Kure Naval Base and nearby airfields on the 24th. Although numerous hits were scored on the cruisers *Tone* and *Oyodo*, neither was sunk. The next day bad weather limited the number of strike groups that made it to their targets. After another fueling retirement on the 26th, Kure was hit again on the 28th with better results because of improved weather. On the 30th, *Yorktown* shifted back to targets in the Tokyo area, hitting airfields and shipping at the Maizuru Naval Base in western Honshu before another fueling retirement and another typhoon kept her out of action until the beginning of August.

Fleet Admiral (as he now was) Nimitz knew but most of the other commanders in the Pacific did not that an atomic bomb was going to be dropped on Hiroshima

The Corsair

The Vought F4U Corsair combined the smallest airframe possible with the most powerful engine then available, the R-2800 Double Wasp, and the combination resembled a "blue baseball bat with wings." Designed before the war, it was the first aircraft to exceed 400 miles per hour in level flight, but its protracted development kept it from operating from aircraft carriers until late in the war. In order to take full advantage of the R-2800's power, a large propeller was needed; that meant an inverted gull wing to provide ground clearance for it, to keep the fuselage at a reasonable ground angle, and to make the length of the landing gear manageable. The gull wing also reduced aerodynamic drag where the wing met the fuselage (at a right angle). A large fuselage fuel tank forced the cockpit to be moved aft in the original design, restricting the pilot's view over the long nose. This change, combined with landing gear problems, made the Corsair difficult to bring aboard a carrier. In time these problems were corrected, but by then the Corsair had become the primary Marine fighter, operating from shore bases, and the Navy had become reluctant to switch from the Hellcat, which had better carrier-landing characteristics. Later in the war the Corsair won a place on board the *Essex*-class carriers when its superior speed was needed to counter the kamikaze threat. The Corsair eventually replaced the Hellcat as the Navy's primary fighter and continued in service into the Korean War as a fighter-bomber.

on 6 August. Nimitz wanted the fleet to be far away from the then-unknown effects of the revolutionary new weapon, and at his order Task Force 38 withdrew from southern Japan. The Japanese government made no declaration that it had accepted the Allied terms for the surrender of all its armed forces as spelled out in the Potsdam Declaration of 26 July. A second atomic bomb was dropped on Nagasaki on 9 August. That day too the Soviet Union declared war on Japan, and its armies swept into Manchuria. Still there was no word from Tokyo. On the 9th and 10th *Yorktown* launched strikes on northern Honshu airfields and on the 13th airfields near Tokyo. After another interlude of fueling and typhoon evasion, *Yorktown* sent her aircraft to hit Tokyo for what was to be the last time on the 15th.

A Japanese ore carrier explodes after attack by *Yorktown* plane off Tsugara, Japan, 30 July 1945. (U.S. Navy)

On that day Japan agreed to capitulate. Remaining strikes planned for that day were canceled. Aircraft already over Japan received a radio message (making reference to *Yorktown*'s call sign): "All Bronco planes cease hostilities and return to base. The war is over." Flights were ordered to jettison their bombs on their way back to the ship. But some diehard Japanese refused to accept surrender. Four *Hancock* Hellcats returning to their ship were attacked by Japanese fighters, but none were lost. Six *Yorktown* Hellcats of VF-88, which had aborted their rocket attack on Atsugi airfield, were intercepted on the way back by an overwhelming number of first-line Japanese pilots in Zeros, Franks, Jacks, Oscars, and Georges. It was a wild melee and the VF-88 pilots put up a valiant fight, but four of the Hellcats went down and their pilots were lost. They would be the last Navy pilots lost in combat during the war. Other Japanese pilots, either uninformed of the surrender or unwilling to accept defeat, continued to attack the fleet; Halsey ordered that they be shot down "in a friendly fashion."

The Third Fleet maintained constant vigilance as preparations for the actual surrender were worked out. Halsey ordered Task Force 38 to a zone known as "Area McCain" 100 to 200 miles southwest of Tokyo. The three task groups maintained their normal wartime patrols through 23 August. On the 16th and 17th, the task force steamed in unusually tight formations for

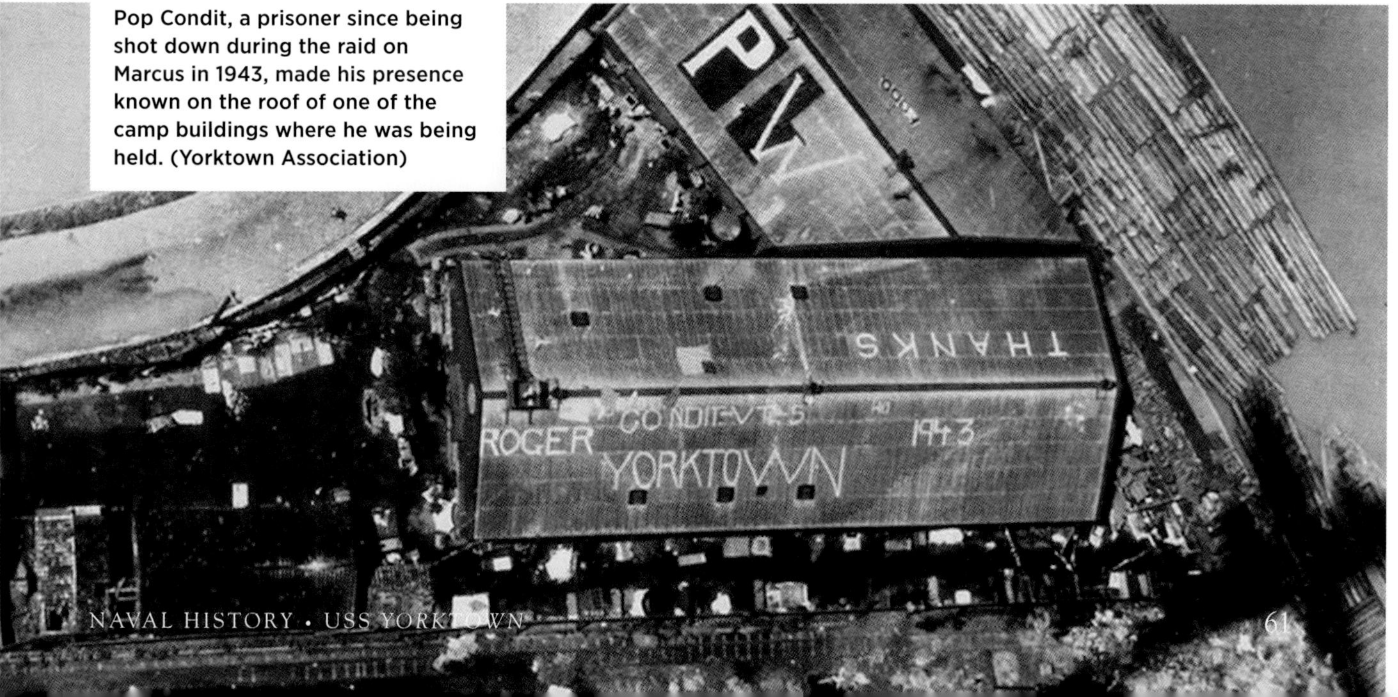

Pop Condit, a prisoner since being shot down during the raid on Marcus in 1943, made his presence known on the roof of one of the camp buildings where he was being held. (Yorktown Association)

commemorative aerial photographs. On the 22nd and 23rd the aircraft took their turn, massing overhead for photographs. On the 23rd, *Yorktown* received orders to head east of Honshu, from where her aircraft provided cover for the occupation forces from the 25th until mid-September. MacArthur had planned to send an advance party to Atsugi to prepare for the arrival of troops from the 11th Airborne Division at the same time Halsey's forces were to land in Yokosuka. Weather postponed all this, but on 27 August a "brash young pilot" from *Yorktown*'s VF-88 landed at Atsugi airfield and ordered the Japanese to put up a banner for the Army paratroopers slated to arrive the next day. It read: "Welcome to the U.S. Army from the Third Fleet."

Before the formal surrender on board the battleship *Missouri* on 2 September, *Yorktown* along with other carriers began air-dropping supplies to Allied prisoners of war in prison camps. They spotted the word "Yorktown" on a roof in one of the camps.

Pop Condit, taken prisoner in 1943, had painted it. Although he had survived the terrible conditions as a prisoner, he and other prisoners had a close call as they were marched toward a canal from where they could be taken out to Halsey's ships in Tokyo Bay. An Avenger flew straight toward them at very low altitude and dropped a fifty-pound bag of sugar, which splattered when it hit the ground. Fortunately, the prisoners scattered when they saw the bomb-bay doors open, and no one was hurt. (Condit, eventually delivered to a hospital ship for medical care and then transferred to a destroyer, was on board *Missouri* during the surrender ceremony.) The carriers continued to drop supplies to prisoner-of-war camps, and members of the ship's company, many of whom had never flown in a plane before, were allowed to ride along as passengers in the Avengers carrying out these missions.

On 16 September, *Yorktown* entered Tokyo Bay with Task Group 38.1, to remain there in upkeep and crew recreation through the end of the month. On 1 October the carrier stood out of Tokyo Bay on her way to Okinawa, arriving in Buckner Bay on 4 October. She loaded passengers on the 5th and got under way for the United States on the 6th. The war was truly over.

Three TBM Avengers of VT-88, 22 August 1945. (U.S. Navy)

THE PEACEFUL YEARS

With the victory won, America immediately began dismantling its military and naval forces and demobilizing personnel. While some were kept on occupation duty, of the three million men and women in naval service at war's end only a half-million remained a year later. The only thing that mattered to most Americans overseas after the war was "getting home."

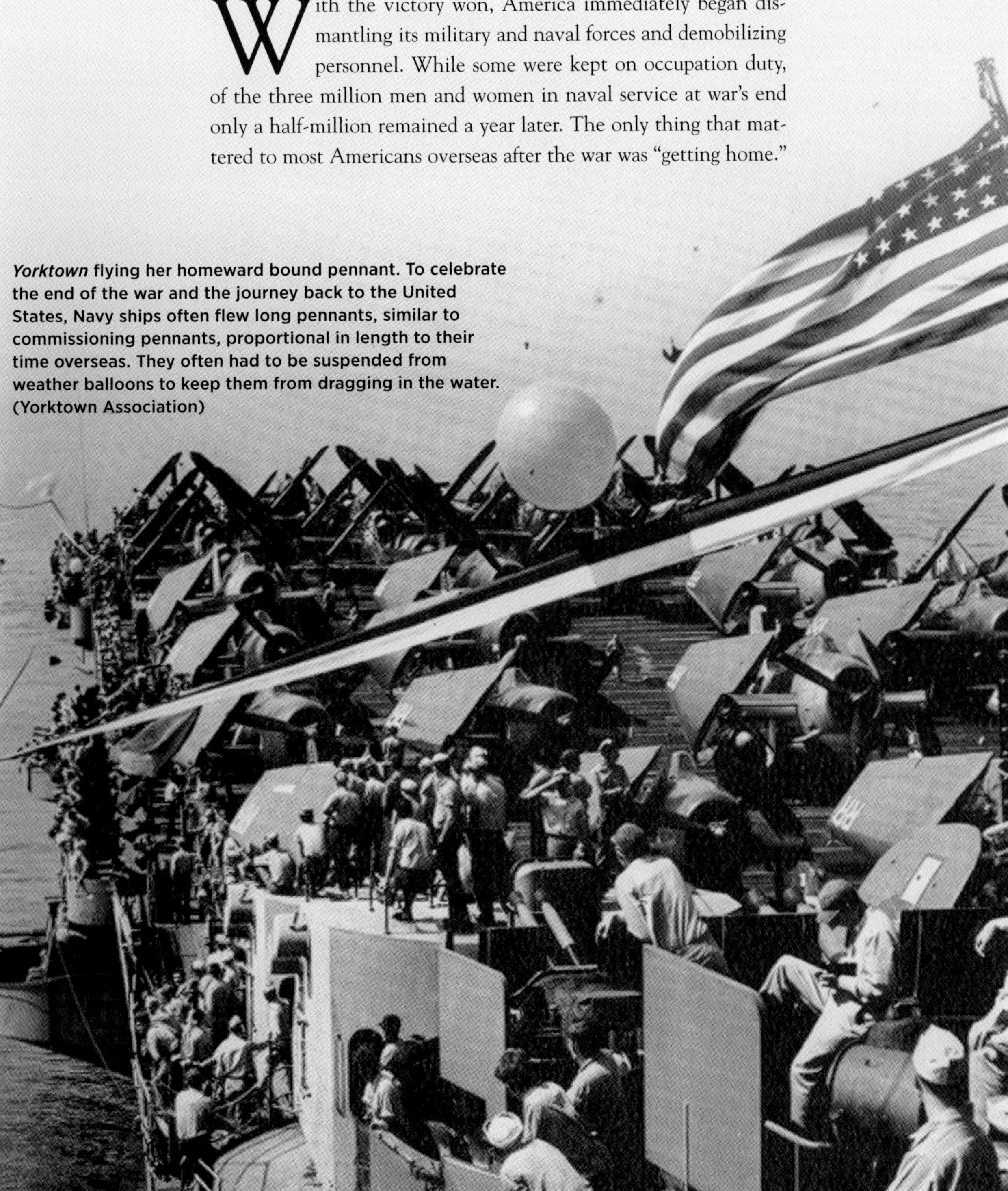

Yorktown flying her homeward bound pennant. To celebrate the end of the war and the journey back to the United States, Navy ships often flew long pennants, similar to commissioning pennants, proportional in length to their time overseas. They often had to be suspended from weather balloons to keep them from dragging in the water. (Yorktown Association)

Yorktown entered San Francisco Bay on 20 October after a nonstop transit. As she passed under the Golden Gate Bridge crowds of people on the span cheered. VF-88 flew overhead, and aviators and crew in dress whites lined the flight deck and spelled out "YORKTOWN" and "FIGHTING LADY." *Yorktown* moored at the Alameda Naval Air Station and discharged her passengers.

On 28 October "Miss Fighting Lady," Betty Jo Copeland, was flown to San Francisco as a guest of the ship's company to accept her title.

She had been selected by a committee of twelve crewmen from more than 1,200 entries submitted to a *Life* magazine contest. A nineteen-year-old brunette from Fort Worth, Texas, she was chosen for her girl-next-door appeal. After being shown around the ship and having lunch with Captain Boone the next day, she attended the ship's victory party held in San Francisco's Civic Auditorium, where she was presented with a watch with the engraved inscription "Miss Fighting Lady," her initials, and "Presented by the U.S.S. *Yorktown*." After the first dance with Captain Boone she danced with crewmen whose names had been drawn. She was given a tour of San Francisco the next day with members of the selection committee, and the day ended with dinner and dancing at the St. Francis Hotel. As she boarded the plane to return home she said, "I've had the most wonderful time of my life."

On 31 October *Yorktown* shifted to Hunters Point Navy Yard for minor repairs. While there she reported to the Service Force, Pacific Fleet for duty with Operation Magic Carpet.

Extra galley facilities were added and tiers of bunks were welded to the hangar deck. On 2 November she

SCB-27A

Yorktown under way after SCB-27A modernization, July 1953. (NHHC)

The Ship Characteristics Board (SCB) was established in 1945 in the office of the Chief of Naval Operations to exert more operational influence on ship-design decisions. Thereafter modernization programs were assigned SCB numbers. Many of these programs applied to aircraft carriers. The SCB-27 modernizations, which could take up to two years for each carrier, allowed operation of the much heavier, faster aircraft of the early jet era. There were two versions of the SCB-27 program. The first, SCB-27A, featured a pair of H-8 hydraulic catapults, and the second, SCB-27C (SCB-27B was canceled) included C-11 steam catapults. *Yorktown* was selected to receive her SCB-27A work starting in June 1952 at the Puget Sound Naval Shipyard and was so reconfigured on recommissioning.

The principal features of SCB-27A were removal of the side-belt armor and its replacement with a hull blister that increased the beam at the waterline to 101 feet; removal of the island's twin 5-inch turrets and addition of four open 5-inch mounts to the starboard side along the edge of the flight deck fore and aft; modifications to the island that replaced the tripod mast with a single pole mast and redesigned the smokestack; strengthening of the flight deck in the landing area; installation of larger and more powerful elevators; replacement of the H4-1 hydraulic catapults with H-8 hydraulic catapults capable of launching aircraft up to 40,000 pounds gross weight; fitting of more powerful bomb and ammunition elevators; provision of equipment for the handling of jet aircraft, including jet-blast deflectors behind the catapults; increase in aviation fuel capacity; installation of higher-capacity aircraft cranes; and subdivision of the hangar deck by two fireproof steel doors. The ready rooms, which had proved vulnerable during the war, were moved from the gallery deck to below the armored hangar deck. To move flight crews in their heavy jet-era gear up to the flight deck, a large escalator was installed on the starboard side below the island.

stood out of San Francisco Bay bound for Guam and arrived in Apra Harbor on the 15th. At Guam Capt. Maurice E. Browder assumed command on 19 November and Captain Boone, newly promoted to rear admiral, left the ship. She got under way with more than 4,000 soldiers as passengers and arrived back in San Francisco on 30 November, to remain there until 8 December, when she headed back to the Far East. Initially bound for Samar in the Philippines, she was diverted to Manila en route, where she arrived on 26 December. She departed there on the 29th with 1,600 soldiers, reaching San Francisco again on 13 January 1946.

Chaplain Joseph Moody introduces "Miss Fighting Lady," Betty Jo Copland. Captain Boone looks on. (U.S. Navy)

Later that month she moved north to Bremerton, Washington, where she was placed "In Commission, In Reserve" on 21 June 1946. To commemorate the event, the crew held a "Final Sortie Dance" that evening at the Field Artillery Armory in Seattle, Washington. On 9 January 1947, *Yorktown* was placed out of commission as part of the Bremerton Group, Pacific Reserve Fleet.

She remained in reserve for almost five years. In June 1952, she was reactivated, and work began to modernize her at the Puget Sound Naval Shipyard in Bremerton, Washington.

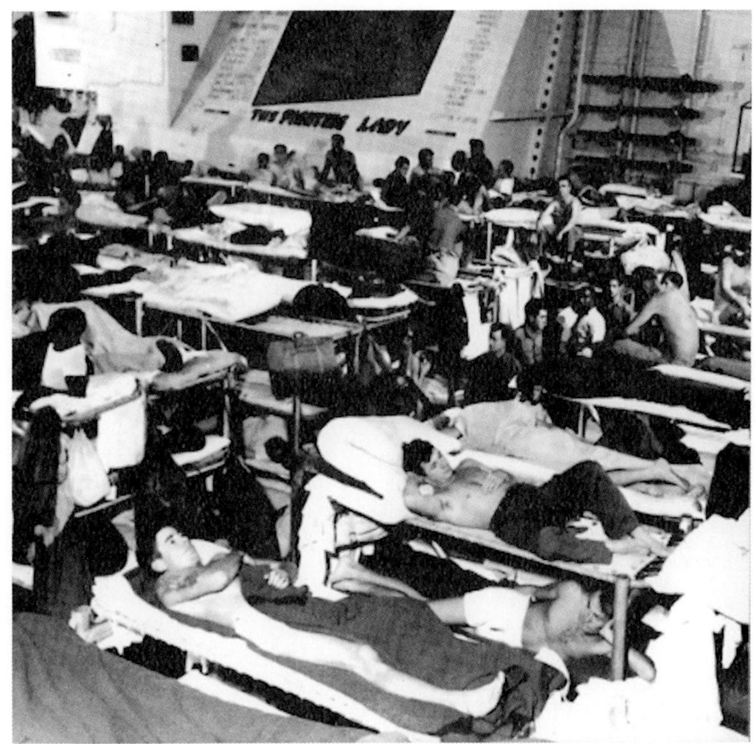

Servicemen returning from the war on board *Yorktown* in Operation Magic Carpet. (Yorktown Association)

As the postwar era unfolded, the Navy struggled to adapt to the growing demands of the Cold War while justifying its continued existence in an age dominated in the public eye by atomic weapons and jet-propelled aircraft. Operating jets from aircraft carriers posed many problems. Jet engines meant speed and high altitude but burned fuel voraciously. The early engines were heavy and produced too little thrust per pound of engine to power load carriers, so the first Navy jet carrier aircraft were all fighters. These aircraft in turn, with their higher gross weights and approach speeds, were more difficult to bring aboard a carrier and, since jet engines took time to "spool up" when power was applied, could not accelerate as quickly as a piston-engine aircraft in case of a waveoff. Also, jets had too little low-speed lift for rolling takeoffs, and launching the heavier jets by catapult strained the capability of the existing H-4 catapults. As early as 1945, the Navy's Bureau of Aeronautics (BuAer) was proposing modifications to the *Essex* class to handle jets. *Yorktown* was chosen for the first of these programs, the SCB-27A, which would allow her to operate safely the latest generation of jet carrier aircraft. On 1 October 1952, while she was still undergoing the associated modernization, she was redesignated as an "attack carrier," CVA, reflecting the Navy's recognition of the primacy of the aircraft carrier in offensive operations. On 15 December 1952, she was placed "In Commission, In Reserve." On completion of her modernization *Yorktown* returned to the active fleet on 20 February 1953, under the command of Capt. William M. Nation.

She spent the next few months off the West Coast working up for her first post–World War II deployment to the western Pacific. In April, men reported on board on temporary duty as "W Division," part of the gunnery department. The five officers, eleven chiefs,

The Bremerton Group of the Pacific Reserve Fleet in Puget Sound, 1948. From foreground, *Essex, Ticonderoga, Yorktown, Lexington, Bunker Hill,* and, in the distant background, *Bon Homme Richard*. (U.S. Navy)

Three-Inch Guns

Toward the end of World War II the Navy sought a more effective antiaircraft weapon. The 3"/50 was developed in 1944 when it was realized that the 20-mm and 40-mm were ineffective in stopping kamikazes. Since a 3-inch projectile was the smallest that could be fitted with a proximity fuse and the concentric recoil spring of the existing 3"/50 lent itself to development of an automatic weapon, a crash program was initiated. The maximum range was under 15,000 yards with an antiaircraft ceiling of over 14,000 feet and a rate of fire from 45 to 50 rounds per minute. With the end of the war development slowed, but by 1948 the 3"/50 was in widespread use throughout the Navy. A twin 3"/50 could fit in the same working circle as a 40-mm quad mount, but since it was heavier, the new mounts usually replaced 40-mm quad mounts on a one-for-three basis. The 3"/50 was included in the SCB-27 program, but as time went on the number of mounts was reduced, as were the 5"/38 weapons, to save weight.

3-inch twin mount. (U.S. Navy)

and eight other enlisted men were in charge of "special ordnance material" (likely atomic weapons) that were part of *Yorktown*'s new role as an attack carrier. Their spaces were guarded by Marines, and their duties were so hush-hush that the crew referred to the group as "the Whispering Division."

On 31 July 1953 Capt. Arnold W. McKechnie relieved Captain Nation (who would later be promoted to rear admiral) before *Yorktown* began her deployment to the western Pacific for a new conflict.

In 1953 several crew members, using spare (if government) parts in their spare time, established a shipboard radio station, the Yorktown Broadcasting Station, and by 1958 YBS was broadcasting on television as well. *Yorktown* also continued her movie career, appearing in the 1954 short documentary *Jet Carrier*, which was nominated for two 1955 Academy Awards, one for Best Documentary, Short Subjects, and one for Best Short Subject, Two-Reel.

Captain Nation congratulates Captain McKechnie on the latter's assumption of command of *Yorktown*, 31 July 1953. (U.S. Navy)

***Yorktown* recommissioning under the command of Capt. William M. Nation, 20 February 1953. Rear Adm. Allen E. Smith, commandant of the Thirteenth Naval District, introduces selected crewmen to the guests. (U.S. Navy)**

ATTACK CARRIER

On 3 August 1953 *Yorktown* left San Francisco under the command of Capt. Arnold W. "Mack" McKechnie, a twenty-six-year Navy veteran who was a qualified submariner as well as a naval aviator.

On her way to Pearl Harbor she embarked Air Group 2. She stayed at Pearl until the 27th before heading for Japan, arriving at Yokosuka on 5 September.

She put to sea again on the 11th to join Task Force 77 in the Sea of Japan as the flagship of Rear Adm. John P. Whitney.

***Yorktown* enters Tokyo Bay for the second time in her career, 5 September 1953. She would operate out of Yokosuka for the next six months as part of Task Force 77. (U.S. Navy)**

Panther about to launch during *Yorktown*'s first deployment to the western Pacific after SCB-27A modernization. Note the raised jet-blast deflector. (U.S. Navy)

***Yorktown*'s flight deck aft showing the centerline elevator, which would be eliminated during her angled-deck modernization. (U.S. Navy)**

The Korean War armistice having been signed two months earlier, *Yorktown* conducted training evolutions rather than combat missions.

Jocko Clark, who had commanded Task Force 77 during the Korean War and had now been promoted vice admiral and to command the Seventh Fleet, flew on board by helicopter to visit the ship at sea.

On 15 December *Yorktown* celebrated the first anniversary of her recommissioning at Yokosuka with the largest cake ever baked on board a Navy vessel—a 1,382-pound replica of the ship—and 150 gallons of ice cream to go with it.

She served with Task Force 77 until February 1954. *Yorktown* stood out of Yokosuka on her way home, stopping at Pearl Harbor en route. She moored at Alameda on 3 March and after a brief repair period at Hunters Point Naval Shipyard put to sea for the filming of the short documentary film *Jet Carrier*. She operated along the West Coast until 1 July and then headed back yet again to the Far East with Air Group 15 on board. She stopped at Pearl Harbor from 8 to 28 July before continuing to Manila, arriving on 4 August, where Capt. Gerald L. Huff relieved Captain McKechnie the next day. *Yorktown* operated out of the Manila–Subic Bay area conducting Seventh Fleet maneuvers for the rest of her deployment, but she did make frequent port visits to Yokosuka and, during the Christmas holidays, a liberty call at Hong Kong.

In February 1955 units of the Seventh Fleet evacuated troops, civilians, and tons of material from the Tachen Islands off the China coast, under attack by communist forces, to Taiwan. Amphibious ships entered the restricted waters off the islands, while the carriers of Task Force 77, *Yorktown*, *Kearsarge*, *Essex*, *Wasp*, and *Midway*, provided air support. *Yorktown* entered Yokosuka for the last time on 16 February but soon departed, on the 18th, for the West Coast. After an overnight stop at Pearl Harbor on 23–24 February, she continued east and arrived at Alameda on 28 February. On 21 March 1955 she was again placed In Commission, In Reserve at the Puget Sound Naval Shipyard for extensive modifications under the SCB-125 program—the changes included an angled flight deck and other improvements.

One of the traditions of carrier aviation is decorating aircraft that land on the wrong carrier by mistake. A "visiting" Cougar from *Oriskany.* (U.S. Navy)

Vice Admiral Clark visits by helicopter at sea, greeted by Captain McKechnie and Rear Admiral Hickey. (U.S. Navy)

An F2H-2P from VC-61 Det A, named like all photo Banshees after illustrated magazines about to launch. The cockpit canopy is open to allow the pilot to escape in a water landing. With better ejection seats this would change. (U.S. Navy)

Yorktown in Hong Kong for Christmas, 1953. Note the original open bow and gun tubs for mounts. (U.S. Navy)

The landing signal officer brings a Cougar on board. The LSO's role would change with the adoption of the angled deck and the mirror landing system. (U.S. Navy)

A Panther of VF-63 waved off by *Yorktown*'s LSO. (U.S. Navy)

Panther

The Grumman F9F Panther was the first Navy jet fighter to see air-to-air combat during the Korean War. It was also the first jet fighter produced by Grumman. The F9F-5 that served on board *Yorktown* was an improved model powered by the Pratt & Whitney J48 engine. The Panther was the basis for the swept-wing F9F variant, the Cougar.

An F2H-3 from VF-23, part of Air Task Group 4 during *Yorktown*'s deployment in 1956. (U.S. Navy)

Banshee

The McDonnell F2H Banshee, originally planned as a day fighter, was notable for its twin Westinghouse J34 engines buried in the wing roots. The first production model, the F2H-1, entered squadron service in 1949. The F2H-2 model, with improved 3,200-pound-thrust J34 engines, flew in combat over Korea. Known affectionately as the "Banjo," the F2H became the Navy's primary jet fighter-bomber and was adapted for a variety of other missions, including photo reconnaissance and night-fighting. The F2H-3 all-weather fighter and F2H-2P photo-reconnaissance versions served on board *Yorktown*.

A HUP-2 from HU-1 Det K during *Yorktown*'s 1956 deployment. (U.S. Navy)

HUP-2

The Piasecki HUP-2 Retriever, a compact, twin-tandem-rotor utility helicopter powered by a 550-horsepower Continental R-975-46 piston engine, was the standard shipboard helicopter for plane guard and utility work on board carriers in the 1950s, replacing the HO3S. It was the first helicopter to have an autopilot to allow hands-off hovering. The HUP-2 version served on board *Yorktown* until the ship's conversion to an ASW carrier in 1958.

Cougars from VF-24 over Pearl Harbor. VF-24 was assigned to Air Group 2 on board *Yorktown* during her western Pacific deployment of 1953–54. (U.S. Navy)

Cougar

The swept-wing Cougar was too late in appearing to see combat during the Korean War but it served for many years in various roles. The F9F-6, powered by a single Pratt & Whitney J48 engine, was primarily a day fighter, and there were light-attack and photo reconnaissance versions as well. Both the F9F-6 and improved F9F-8 served on board *Yorktown*, as did the photo reconnaissance variant.

Skyraider

The separate dive-bomber and torpedo aircraft of World War II were ultimately replaced by a single attack aircraft, the Douglas AD Skyraider. The Skyraider was a single-seat, piston-engine aircraft that had the performance of a World War II fighter and the ability to carry an amazing amount of ordnance. The "Able Dog" was powered by a 2,700-horsepower Wright R-3350 radial engine and was armed with four 20-mm cannon in the wings. The Skyraider, described as a "dump truck with wings," performed a variety of roles. Special-mission-configured aircraft were identified by suffixes added to the basic designation: *N* for all-weather, *W* for radar surveillance, or *Q* for electronic countermeasures. It served during the Vietnam War as the A-1, or as it was affectionately known, the "Spad."

An AD-4 Skyraider from VA-65 taxies over the barricade, dropped between launches. (U.S. Navy)

HO3S-1

The Sikorsky HO3S-1 was the Navy version of the Air Force H-5. Although its designation indicated an observation helicopter, the HO3S-1 was also used for utility, mercy missions, and rescue, as well as, in its extensive service in the Korean War, specifically combat rescue—the recovery of pilots shot down behind enemy lines. Powered by a Pratt & Whitney R-985 Wasp Junior radial engine of 450 horsepower, it carried a pilot and three passengers. It was used in active service until 1957, when it was replaced by newer models.

The HO3S-1, the Navy version of the Sikorsky H-5. (U.S. Navy)

A NEW AGE

A VA-216 Skyraider and a VF-214 Cougar, 1956. (U.S. Navy)

Yorktown completed her conversion in the fall of 1955 and on 14 October was placed back in commission under Capt. Emmett O'Beirne. She carried out local operations along the West Coast until mid-March 1956. On the 19th, she stood out of San Francisco Bay for her third deployment with the Seventh Fleet. On board was Air Task Group 4 (ATG-4). (The air task group was a type of air group during the 1950s composed of squadrons temporarily collected from standing air groups.)

Yorktown remained at Pearl Harbor from 24 March to 9 April and then continued westward, arriving in Yokosuka, Japan, on the 18th. She left there on the 29th and operated with the Seventh Fleet for the next five months.

Those months took her to the Sea of Japan, the East China Sea, the South China Sea, Sasebo, Manila, Subic Bay, and Buckner Bay in Okinawa.

On 7 September, she departed Yokosuka and headed east, arriving at Alameda on 13 September after a nonstop voyage. Capt. Edward E. Colestock assumed command on the 14th and *Yorktown* resumed West Coast operations for about two months. On 13 November, she made a round trip to Pearl Harbor, returning to Alameda on 11 December. There followed local operations out of Alameda, which included training exercises in local and frequent in port visits for upkeep and repair, until March 1957.

On 19 March she departed Alameda for another tour of duty in the western Pacific, this time with Air Group 19, making stops at Oahu and Guam along the way and arriving at Yokosuka on 19 April.

She put to sea on 25 April to join Task Force 77 and operated with it for the next three months.

On 13 August 1957, *Yorktown* left Yokosuka for the last time, making a brief stop at Pearl Harbor before arriving at Alameda on the 25th. On 1 September *Yorktown* was reclassified as an ASW aircraft carrier, hull number CVS-10, and began the next phase of her naval career.

The flight-deck crew rigging the barricade, 1956. The barricades used in World War II were ineffective in the postwar jet era and were replaced by new barriers that could be raised as needed. (U.S. Navy)

An LSO, 1956. The officer behind him is likely the squadron LSO. (U.S. Navy)

The barricade in action. A Cougar of VF-94 is brought to a halt during an emergency recovery, 1956. (U.S. Navy)

Yorktown **alongside the store ship** ***Pictor*** **(AF-54), 1957. Note the SCB-125 enclosed ("hurricane") bow. The destroyer** ***Bausell*** **(DD-845) is on** ***Pictor*****'s starboard side. (U.S. Navy)**

SCB-125

A major British innovation for aircraft carriers was the angled deck, a simple but revolutionary concept that allowed aircraft to "go around" without hitting the barricade protecting other aircraft forward. The Navy began to give the angled-deck concept serious consideration in 1951 and in the spring of 1952 gave two carriers, the large carrier *Midway* and the *Essex*-class *Wasp* superficial modifications to test the concept. Later *Antietam*, an essentially unmodified *Essex*-class "straight-deck" unit, became the Navy's first true angled-deck carrier.

Angled decks were applied to the *Essex* class under the SCB-125 program, which also fit an enclosed "hurricane" bow. *Yorktown* received her SCB-125 modernization from February to October 1955 at the Puget Sound Naval Shipyard.

The mirror landing system was another British innovation. To take advantage of the capabilities offered by the angled deck a new method of controlling aircraft as they approached had to be devised, since a landing signal officer could only control one aircraft at a time and the limitations of the human eye limited control using paddles to no more than one-half mile. The British had another simple and elegant solution. The system placed a large mirror, concave around its horizontal axis, alongside the landing area at the edge of the angled deck, pointed astern. The mirror was aligned with the angle of the glide path and mounted on gimbals connected to the ship's fire-control system, which was gyro stabilized. This allowed the mirror to compensate for any movement of the ship. Aft of the mirror was a powerful light source, from which the mirror reflected a cone of light back up the glide slope. The pilot would see it as a spot of light, the "ball," when he was in the middle of the beam. A horizontal row of green datum lights mounted on either side of the mirror helped him position the aircraft. If the pilot was a little high on the glide path, the ball appeared slightly above the reference lights and if too low, below the reference lights. Later, the mirror was replaced by a Fresnel lens and colors were added to the ball, but the principle was the same. These modifications allowed the aircraft carrier truly to enter the jet age.

Yorktown **as configured by SCB-125. (U.S. Navy)**

Fury

The North American FJ-1 Fury was the straight-winged progenitor of the famous F-86 Sabre. The follow-on FJ-2 was essentially a navalized Sabre with folding wings, a longer nose strut for increased angle of attack at launch, and beefed-up landing gear for the hard landings on carrier decks. It was also armed with four 20-mm cannons instead of the Sabre's six .50-caliber machine guns. The version that flew from the *Yorktown* was the FJ-3, powered by the Wright J65, a license-built version of the British Armstrong Siddeley Sapphire.

FJ-3 from VF-191 on *Yorktown* as part of Air Group 19, 1957. (NNAM)

The 5-inch and 3-inch batteries on *Yorktown*'s port bow in preparations for her 1957 deployment. (U.S. Navy)

An AJ-2 Savage from VAH-6 Det E moving into position on the catapult. (U.S. Navy)

ANTISUBMARINE CARRIER

***Yorktown*'s first deployment as an ASW carrier, 1958–59. (U.S. Navy)**

Reclassified as an antisubmarine warfare carrier and assigned a new homeport in Alameda, *Yorktown* entered Puget Sound Naval Shipyard on 27 September 1957 for overhaul and ASW modifications. By the beginning of February she had left the yard period for the naval ammunition depot at Bangor, Washington, until the 7th. She entered Long Beach five days later. For the next eight months *Yorktown* conducted local operations along the West Coast.

On 1 November she left San Diego for her first deployment to the western Pacific in her new role, under the command of Capt. Porter F. Bedell. After a stop at Pearl Harbor from the 8th to the 17th, *Yorktown* continued westward and arrived in Yokosuka on the 25th. On board was Rear Adm. Edward E. Colestock, commander, Carrier Division 17 (ComCarDiv 17).

Antisubmarine Carrier Air Groups (CVSGs) would be established later (see sidebar next page), but for now an ad hoc selection of squadrons embarked on *Yorktown*: VS-37 flying the S2F-1/2 Tracker, HS-2 flying the HSS-1 Seabat, VF-92 Detachment N with the F2H-3 Banshee, and VAW-11 Detachment N with the AD-5W Skyraider.

In December 1958 *Yorktown* and eight other ships of her ASW group were diverted from operations at sea to aid the people of Koniya, Amami O-Shima Island, in the South China Sea between Kyushu and Okinawa, left homeless by a fire that swept through the town and destroyed most of its dwellings. Within twenty-four hours of the disaster the group delivered food,

F2H-3 Banshee from VF-92 Det N, *Yorktown*'s 1958–59 deployment. (U.S. Navy)

An S2F "Stoof" from VS-37 aboard Yorktown during her 1958–59 deployment. (U.S. Navy)

medicines, clothing, blankets, and tents to the affected citizens and continued until Japanese relief agencies could cope with the situation.

During this deployment *Yorktown* qualified for three Armed Forces Expeditionary Medals. The first was for the period 31 December to 1 January 1959, when she was part of an American show of force in response to communist Chinese shelling of offshore islands, Quemoy and Matsu, held by the Chinese Nationalists. During January she joined contingency forces off South Vietnam in the U.S. response to internal disorder there caused by communist guerrilla activity. That month she earned a third medal for service in the Taiwan Strait. Otherwise, except for another visit to Vietnamese waters late in March, *Yorktown* carried out normal training evolutions and port visits. On 15 April *Yorktown* sailed from Singapore with thirty British Commonwealth, American, and French warships for a Southeast Asia Treaty Organization (SEATO) naval exercise. (SEATO was founded in 1954 by the United States, France, Great Britain, New Zealand, Australia, the Philippines, Thailand, and Pakistan to deter communist expansion in the region. SEATO was dissolved in 1977 due to disagreements among its member nations over the Vietnam War.)

Her deployment ending at San Diego on 21 May, *Yorktown* resumed local operations along the West

ASW Carrier Groups

Antisubmarine Carrier Air Groups, CVSGs, were established in 1960–61 and numbered between 50 and 60. These formations continued to be called air *groups* even after the attack carrier air groups were retitled as *wings*, CVWs, in 1963. An antisubmarine air group included two VS fixed-wing antisubmarine squadrons flying the S-2 Tracker, an HS helicopter antisubmarine squadron equipped with SH-3 Sea King helicopters, and a VAW airborne early warning (AEW) squadron with E-1 Tracers. Operating in the Pacific and Atlantic, the antisubmarine carriers monitored the growing Soviet submarine force, and as ASW gained in importance, the ships themselves were again modernized, this time under a Navy-wide program known as Fleet Rehabilitation and Modernization II. SCB-144 was the FRAM II modernization aimed at improving the ASW capabilities of the SCB-27A CVS carriers. The principal modifications included the installation of a bow-mounted sonar dome for the SQS-23 sonar, a stem hawsepipe for the bow anchor (to clear the sonar dome), and modifications to the Combat Information Center. By 1965 all the FRAM II conversions were back in service.

Coast for the rest of 1959, now under Capt. Louis H. Bauer. On 4 January 1960 *Yorktown* began her next deployment, under Capt. Charles E. Gibson, this time with VS-25, HS-4, and Detachment T from VAW-11. Rear Adm. Joseph D. Black was riding as ComCarDiv 17. During this short deployment *Yorktown* earned additional Armed Forces Expeditionary Medals for duty in Vietnamese waters in March, April, May, and June. Returning to the West Coast in late summer, *Yorktown* began in late September a four-month overhaul at Puget Sound, to 27 January 1961.

Yorktown next conducted refresher training and local operations until late July, when she began her third deployment as a CVS, this time under Capt. William G. Privette Jr. This time she was assigned a formal ASW air group, CVSG-55: two Tracker squadrons, VS-23 and VS-25, along with HS-4 and VAW-11 Detachment T. During this deployment, from late July to early March 1962, Rear Adm. James O. Cobb, ComCarDiv 19, was the embarked flag officer. (Cobb had previously been *Yorktown*'s captain, when she was an attack carrier.) In addition to various antiair and antisubmarine warfare exercises *Yorktown* made numerous port calls in Japan and visits to Okinawa, the Philippines, and Hong Kong. In October *Yorktown* had to deal with a typhoon. Her deployment ended at Long Beach on 2 March 1962. She conducted local operations through the summer and into the fall.

But first came a special tasking. On 27 April *Yorktown* left Long Beach with three destroyers as part of the launch surveillance unit during Operation Dominic I, the last atmospheric tests of nuclear weapons by the United States. These tests included high-altitude detonations at Johnston Island, air-dropped airbursts near Johnston and Christmas Islands, an airburst near Christmas Island delivered by a Polaris missile fired by a nuclear ballistic-missile submarine (SSBN), and an underwater test off the West Coast.

On 26 October 1962 *Yorktown* left Long Beach under Capt. Waller C. Moore on her fourth deployment, Rear Adm. Joseph A. Jaap, ComCarDiv 19, embarked. She participated in a number of antisubmarine and air warfare exercises, including the SEATO ASW exercise Operation Sea Serpent in May. In June 1963 she completed her deployment and began a major overhaul at Long Beach that lasted until June of the following year. Then followed local operations for the rest of the year under Capt. James P. Lynch.

On 23 October 1964, under Capt. Raymond S. "Gus" Osterhoudt, with Rear Adm. Kenneth L Veth riding as commander, Anti-Submarine Warfare Group 3, *Yorktown* departed on another deployment to the western Pacific. This time she became a participant in the war in Vietnam, in which America's involvement was growing.

An S2F Tracker from VS-25. (U.S. Navy)

Tracker

The Grumman S2F Tracker, a large aircraft powered by two 1,525-horsepower Wright R-1820 radial engines, was the Navy's first purpose-built carrier antisubmarine aircraft. It could accommodate both search equipment, such as radar and MAD (Magnetic Anomaly Detection) gear, and attack weapons in the form of depth charges and homing torpedoes. Known as "Stoofs," Trackers first deployed with squadrons in early 1954 and were larger than any other carrier aircraft at the time except the AJ-1 Savage. The Tracker was redesignated as the S-2 in 1962 and served aboard antisubmarine warfare carriers until the 1970s.

Tracer

From the Tracker the Navy developed, with a larger fuselage, the TF-1 Trader as a "carrier onboard delivery" (COD) aircraft. The Trader was later redesignated as the C-1. The WF Tracer, often called the "Willy Fudd," was developed from the Trader for AEW. The aircraft featured a large streamlined radome (housing in which an antenna could rotate) atop the fuselage for the AN/APS-82 radar. Inevitably, since the S2F was the Stoof, the Tracer became the "Stoof with a roof." With a detection radius out to 250 to 300 miles, the Tracer, soon redesignated as the E-1, saw extensive service during the early years of the Vietnam War, providing early warning of enemy aircraft activity to strike aircraft.

A VAW-11 E-1B Tracer. (Hancock Association)

Seabat

The Sikorsky HSS-1 Seabat was a piston-engine helicopter originally designed for antisubmarine warfare and embarked in *Yorktown* air groups. It was adopted by the Army as the H-34 and saw extensive service in Vietnam. Other versions saw service with the Marines, the Coast Guard, and the armed forces of twenty-five countries. It was redesignated SH-34 in 1962.

An HSS-1 Seabat from HS-2 during *Yorktown*'s 1958–59 western Pacific deployment. (U.S. Navy)

Sea King

The Sikorsky Sea King was originally designated as the HSS-2, though it was entirely a new design, not an HSS-1 follow-on. The Sea King combined the roles of hunter and killer, which had previously been carried out by two variants of the HSS-1. Redesignated as the SH-3 in 1962, the Sea King performed many other roles as well, such as search and rescue, transport, antishipping, medical evacuation, plane guard, and airborne early warning. It ended service with the Navy in 2006 but continues to be popular with foreign military and civilian operators.

An SH-3 Sea King from HS-4. (U.S. Navy)

VIETNAM

Yorktown leaves Long Beach for Vietnam, 1964. (U.S. Navy)

During the Vietnam War the Navy's CVSs performed vital if relatively inconspicuous services for the attack carriers involved in the conflict. As *Yorktown*'s 1966 cruise book eloquently put it:

> This book is not about a ship.
> This book is about men.
> Without men a ship is merely inert machinery.
> Many of these men are husbands and fathers who would like to be home with their families.
> Many of these men have sweethearts who would like to spend more time with them.
> These men are sons and brothers who would like to spend the summer on vacation with their folks.
> But in this time of crisis, as in time of peace, these men had an important assignment that took them from their homes.
> Their assignment was not exciting and glamorous.
> Their assignment was usually hot and often boring, but vital.
> It was vital to the cold, wet pilot under fire, waiting to be rescued from the approaching enemy junks.
> It was vital to the remainder of the Navy off Vietnam who needed to know what was on and under the sea about them.
> This book is about that assignment and how professionally these men handled it.
> This book is about the men of "The Fighting Lady" on station off Vietnam in 1966.

On 22 October 1964 *Yorktown* headed west again for duty with the Seventh Fleet. After operating off Hawaii until early December she began her first real involvement in the Vietnam War.

In February, March, and April she was in the South China Sea off Vietnam in antisubmarine and rescue support for the fast carriers flying air strikes against targets in, especially, North Vietnam.

An addition to her air group was a detachment of A-4 Skyhawks from Marine Attack Squadron 223 (VMA-223) to act as "fighters" to provide her some degree of air and surface defense.

Operation Rolling Thunder, a series of continuous retaliatory strikes against North Vietnam, had begun in February 1965 and would go on for three years.

In March, after thirty days of continuous operation, *Yorktown* took part with Task Force 77 in Operation Candid Camera—i.e., an official photograph.

She departed Yokosuka to return to the West Coast, arriving at Long Beach on the 17th. On 5 January 1966, after seven months of local operations out of Long Beach, *Yorktown* got under way for the western Pacific again.

This time her air group would again include A-4's, with the same tasks, but this time they were a detachment from a unit, Anti-Submarine Fighter Squadron 1 (VSF-1), the Navy specially created for the purpose. Also, the E-1B Tracer replaced the EA-1E in the airborne early warning role.

An SH-3 Sea King from HS-4 in ASW exercises with a friendly submarine. (U.S. Navy)

(above) Marine A-4C Skyhawks from VMA-223 Det T embarked on *Yorktown* for her first tour in the Vietnam War as defensive "fighters" to protect her if needed. For her next deployment she would have a detachment of A-4B Skyhawks from VSF-1. (U.S. Navy)

(right) Hooking up the catapult "bridle" for an EA-1E of VAW-11 Det T prior to launch. (U.S. Navy)

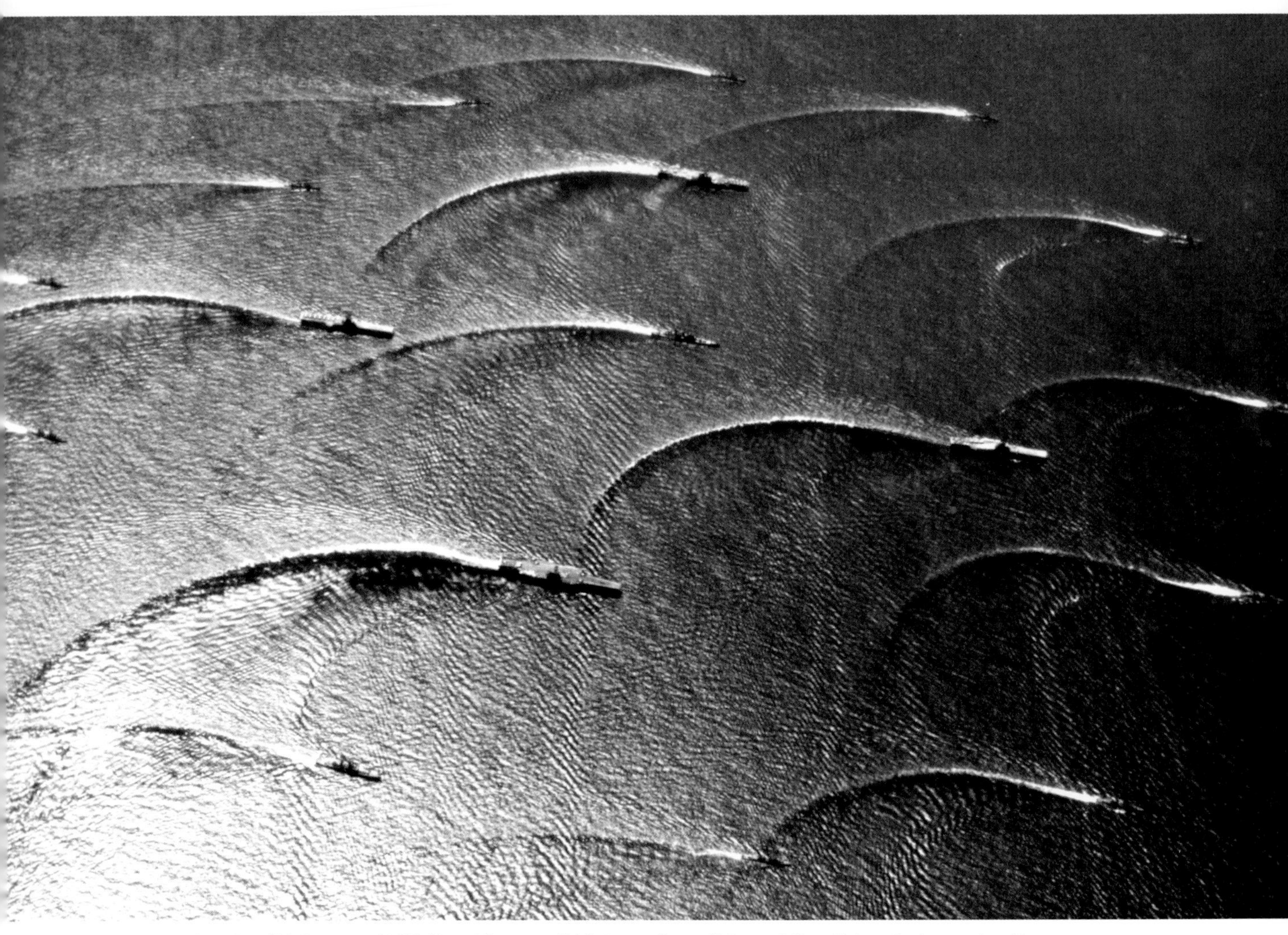

Operation Candid Camera, 1965: Naval forces off Vietnam "pose" for public-affairs photographs. *Ranger* appears toward the bottom, *Yorktown* off her port quarter. The other carriers are (clockwise from *Yorktown*) *Coral Sea* and *Hancock*. (U.S. Navy)

She arrived in Yokosuka on 17 February and joined Task Force 77 on Yankee Station, a point in the Gulf of Tonkin from which Rolling Thunder strikes were flown, later that month.

On 12 March, Ann-Margret visited the ship with Johnny Rivers and his band. The crew spelled out "Hi Annie!" in formation on the flight deck, and the Marine Detachment provided an honor guard through which she walked with Capt. James Cain on her arrival.

Over the next five months *Yorktown* was "on the line" on Yankee Station three times providing antisubmarine and rescue services for the carriers of Task Force 77. She also participated in several ASW exercises, including a major SEATO exercise, Operation Sea Imp. Ending her last tour on Yankee Station in early July, *Yorktown* headed home, after a stop at Yokosuka. She disembarked her air group at San Diego on 27 July and arrived at Long Beach the same day. *Yorktown* conducted local operations, carrier qualifications, and exercises for the rest of the year and the first two months of 1967. On 24 February 1967 *Yorktown* entered the Long Beach Naval Shipyard for a seven-month overhaul, completed early in October. After refresher training, she resumed local West Coast operations for most of the rest of 1967.

On 28 December she stood out of Long Beach for what would be her last tour of duty in the western Pacific. She arrived in the Far East late in January 1968 after a stop at Pearl Harbor, but world events intervened and she was diverted, along with other naval forces, to the Sea of Japan in response to the North Korean seizure of the intelligence-gathering ship *Pueblo* in January. *Yorktown* provided ASW and search and rescue (SAR) support for the contingency forces.

She operated there for a month before being released on 1 March, after which she headed for Subic Bay in the Philippines. Thereafter *Yorktown* did another three line periods on Yankee Station with Task Force 77 in support of the attack carriers.

She ended her deployment on 16 June and headed for Yokosuka, where she stopped from 19 to 21 June before heading back to West Coast. She entered the Long Beach Naval Shipyard on 5 July for almost three months of repairs, which were completed at the end of September 1968. Local operations followed, but they were to be her last in the Pacific before transfer to the Atlantic Fleet—after, that is, participating in some interesting evolutions. In the first she was a backdrop for an episode of the television comedy series *Get Smart*, and in the second she served as a platform for the filming of the movie *Tora! Tora! Tora!* depicting the attack on Pearl Harbor. As her final act in the Pacific *Yorktown* served as a recovery ship for the Apollo 8 space mission.

An E-1B Tracer from VAW11, 1966. (U.S. Navy)

***Pueblo* (AGER-2), captured off North Korea in the Sea of Japan, 23 January 1968. *Yorktown* was a part of the naval force that responded. *Pueblo* is still on display in Pyongyang as a museum ship. (U.S. Navy)**

Pueblo

The *Pueblo* (AGER-2) was classified as an environmental research ship but was used to gather intelligence and oceanographic information off North Korea while operating in international waters in the Sea of Japan. On 23 January 1968 she was forcibly captured by North Korean air and naval forces. *Pueblo* could not outrun her attackers and had no effective means of defense. One crew member died during the capture and eighty-two others were taken prisoner. Tortured and beaten, deprived of adequate food and medical care, the crew was forced to write confessions and were told that they would be tried as spies. The crew spent the next eleven months in captivity while the U.S. tried to get them released through diplomatic means. The crew was finally released on 23 December 1968 but the *Pueblo* is still held by North Korea and is on display in Pyongyang as a museum ship.

(top) An S-2E from VS-25. Note the unique wing-folding method. (U.S. Navy)

(left) An S-2 from VS-25 with MAD boom extended and rockets on its wing pylons. (U.S. Navy)

(bottom) The CVSs monitored surface contacts, rescued downed airmen, and tracked potential submarine threats. HS-4 Sea Kings overfly a surfaced Whiskey-class submarine. (U.S. Navy)

Yorktown with her flight deck painted for her portrayal of the Japanese carrier *Akagi* during the filming of *Tora! Tora! Tora!* (NNAM)

LAST DAYS IN THE PACIFIC

GET SMART

Yorktown arrived back in Long Beach on 5 July 1968 and entered the Long Beach Naval Shipyard the same day for repairs. There Capt. John G. Fifield assumed command. The repairs were completed on 30 September and *Yorktown* resumed local operations. On the 16th and 17th of October *Yorktown* hosted the cast and crew of the television comedy series *Get Smart*, starring Don Adams as "Agent Maxwell Smart," Barbara Felden as "Agent 99," and Ed Platt as "Chief of Control." The episode, "Temporarily Out of Control" from the fourth season of the show, revolved around Max and Agent 99 being prevented from going on their honeymoon by Max and the Chief being recalled to active duty. Scenes were shot with the carrier's island as background and on the hangar deck. Between takes and during breaks *Yorktown*'s crew took pictures of, and posed for photos with, the cast, collected autographs, and asked questions about show business.

The television crew were not the only visitors during this time. The next occasion turned out less happily. On 23 November a Dependents Day cruise was scheduled, but after the wives and kids were already on board Captain Fifield had to cancel getting under way; dense smog in the Los Angeles area had greatly reduced visibility. The next is still remembered today.

Ed Platt as "Chief of Control" explains the situation to Don Adams as "Agent Maxwell Smart" in the *Get Smart* episode "Temporarily Out of Control," filmed on board *Yorktown*. (U.S. Navy)

TORA! TORA! TORA!

Yorktown was given a role in the very popular 1970 film *Tora! Tora! Tora!*, depicting the attack on Pearl Harbor—none other than one of the attacking Japanese carriers, *Akagi* (which had been sunk at Midway). In preparing for her portrayal, the stripes on *Yorktown*'s angled deck were painted over and altered to resemble *Akagi*'s straight deck.

On 2 December, 30 Zero, Kate, and Val look-alikes, converted AT-6 and BT-13 trainers, were hoisted on board *Yorktown* at North Island Naval Air Station. The ship got under way that night.

Off San Diego at 0600 *Yorktown* turned into the wind to launch the "Japanese" aircraft so they could be filmed taking off. Many of the flight-deck crew visible in the scene were costumed in Japanese naval uniforms of that era.

These aircraft flew back not to *Yorktown* but to North Island, since they were not actual carrier aircraft and did not have arresting gear.

Yorktown returned to North Island to load the "Japanese" aircraft again and proceeded to Pearl Harbor for the next phase of filming, arriving on 10 December. There *Yorktown* berthed next to the Arizona Memorial and unloaded her disguised trainers before preparing for her next significant event, assignment as the recovery ship for the Apollo 8 space mission.

Film crew on board *Yorktown* for *Tora! Tora! Tora!* (U.S. Navy)

A Credited Movie Role

Tora! Tora! Tora! dramatizes the events leading up to and during the Japanese attack on Pearl Harbor in 1941, from both the American and Japanese viewpoints. After three years in production, the film was released in the United States on 23 September 1970 and in Japan two days later. It was praised for its historical accuracy and attention to detail, its visual effects, and its action sequences. The film was created in two separate productions, one based in the United States and one based in Japan, with ensemble casts of both American and Japanese actors, some not trained actors but authentic in appearance. Scale ship models were used for many of the overhead shots, and some of them were full-scale mockups in the Japanese-produced sequences.

The 23 November 1968 Dependents Day cruise was canceled because of dense smog from Los Angeles. The dependents were already on board, however, and had a chance to explore the ship. (U.S. Navy)

A "Kate" launching from "*Akagi*" for *Tora! Tora! Tora!* (U.S. Navy)

Yorktown flight-deck personnel costumed as Japanese sailors for *Tora! Tora! Tora!* (U.S. Navy)

APOLLO 8

Off Hawaii from 16 December on, media representatives on board *Yorktown* observed the crew in recovery exercises with a mockup Apollo 8 capsule. The spacecraft splashed down on 27 December at 0452 a thousand miles southwest of Hawaii but only two and a half miles from *Yorktown*. The parachutes and flashing light on the capsule could be seen from the ship. The first helicopter, from HS-4 on *Yorktown*, with three swimmers from Underwater Demolition Team 12, arrived 43 minutes (having waited for daylight) after splashdown to attach sea anchors and a floatation collar.

Forty-five minutes later, the Apollo 8 crew was safely on the flight deck. Frank Borman had requested that an electric razor be on the recovery helicopter, and he used it on the way in to the ship. He was very clean shaven when he stepped on board *Yorktown*, in contrast to his crewmates, who each sported a week's growth of beard.

Captain Fifield welcoming the Apollo 8 astronauts on board. (NHHC)

Frogmen from UDT-12 attaching the floatation collar to the Apollo 8 capsule. (NASA)

The Apollo 8 crew, astronauts Frank Borman, William Anders, and James Lovell, arriving on *Yorktown*. (NASA)

Men of the Year

Apollo 8 was launched on 21 December 1968 as the first human spaceflight from the Kennedy Space Center, Cape Kennedy, Florida. The capsule took 68 hours to travel to the Moon and over the course of 20 hours orbited the Moon ten times, during which the crew made a Christmas Eve television broadcast reading from the Book of Genesis. It was the first crewed spacecraft to leave Earth and the first human spaceflight to reach the Moon. Air Force colonel Frank Borman, Navy captain James Lovell, and Air Force major William Anders were the first humans to witness and photograph the far side of the Moon and an earthrise. The Apollo 8 astronauts returned to Earth on 27 December 1968, when their spacecraft splashed down in the Pacific Ocean. The crew members were named *Time* magazine's "Men of the Year" for 1968 upon their return. Apollo 8 paved the way for the eventual landing on the Moon by Apollo 11 in 1969.

They were first greeted by the senior member of the NASA recovery team, John Stoneifer. Then Captain Fifield welcomed the astronauts on board.

After a few brief words by Frank Borman, who thanked the crew for giving up Christmas to await their splashdown, the astronauts rode the elevator down to the hangar deck and proceeded immediately to the sick bay for four hours of medical tests by the NASA medical team, interrupted by breakfast and a telephone conversation with President Lyndon B. Johnson. After lunch with Captain Fifield in his inport cabin (much larger and more pleasant than his sea cabin in the island) the astronauts spent the afternoon debriefing. After a formal dinner in the wardroom they met the crew on the hangar deck for a reenlistment ceremony and a cake cutting. The next morning there were more medical tests in sickbay and a brunch in the chiefs' mess before flying off to Hawaii, where they caught another flight to Houston. The capsule was on board *Yorktown* when she arrived in Hawaii on 29 December.

Yorktown's year ended with transfer to the Atlantic for what would the twilight of her career.

The Apollo 8 capsule hoisted on board *Yorktown*. (NASA)

TWILIGHT

***Yorktown* entering Valparaiso, Chile, 31 January 1969. (U.S. Navy)**

Departing Pearl Harbor on 2 January 1969, *Yorktown* stopped at Long Beach for two weeks before continuing her voyage to join the Atlantic Fleet. When *Yorktown* left Long Beach three prominent civilians from the Navy League, including the national director, Robert B. Smith, went on board for the trip around Cape Horn. *Yorktown* crossed the equator on the 27th en route to Valparaiso, Chile, and many of her crew became shellbacks, as is the tradition among sailors. She arrived in Valparaiso, Chile, on 31 January. As she entered the harbor she rendered a 21-gun salute in honor of the president of Chile, followed by a 13-gun salute for the commandant of the First Naval Zone. The salutes were answered by Chilean shore batteries, which made for an impressive arrival.

On the first day in Valparaiso she was visited by the governor, the mayors of Valparaiso and nearby Vina del Mar, and ranking Chilean naval officers. During her three-day visit *Yorktown* hosted nearly 11,000 visitors, who were shown displays that included the Apollo 8 "boilerplate" practice capsule. Many crew members were given tours by the Chilean navy, and *Yorktown* delivered five tons of "Handclasp" material that included clothing, medicines, and sporting equipment to be distributed by the U.S. Naval Mission in Chile. The crew also competed in golf and basketball against Chilean navy teams but lost in both sports.

After her departure many *Yorktown* crew members considered Valparaiso to be the friendliest port they had visited. On her second day out of Valparaiso *Yorktown* was refueled at sea by the Chilean fleet oiler *Almirante Jorge Montt*, allowing her to continue on her way around Cape Horn.

Refueling from the Chilean fleet oiler *Almirante Jorge Montt*. (U.S. Navy)

Yorktown rounds Cape Horn. (U.S. Navy)

Captain Fifield greeting Admiral Clark, retired. (U.S. Navy)

In the evening of 7 February all *Yorktown* crew members became mossbacks, another traditional rite for sailors, marking their ship's rounding of the southernmost tip of South America.

Her next port of call was Rio de Janeiro, Brazil. She arrived on Valentine's Day, 14 February, the day before Rio's annual four-day celebration of Carnival, and anchored in Guanabara Bay. Although business in Rio comes to a standstill as costumed groups and bands parade and celebrate, almost a thousand visitors were on board *Yorktown* during her stay, and nearly seven tons of Handclasp material was off-loaded.

Departing on the 17th *Yorktown* arrived at her new home port in Norfolk, Virginia, on the 28th. As she arrived fireboats greeted her with streams of water played in the air.

Her crew manned the rails as she moored alongside the attack carrier *John F. Kennedy*. Dependents boarded after the ship tied up, and Captain Fifield, after greeting Rear Adm. Charles S. Minter Jr., ComCarDiv 16, also greeted retired Admiral Clark, *Yorktown*'s first skipper. It had been 26 years since she had last been in Norfolk.

Yorktown conducted operations in the Caribbean and western Atlantic until late summer. In June *Yorktown* participated in the NATO antisubmarine warfare exercise Operation Spark Plug in the West Indies along with ships of the navies of Canada, Great Britain, the Netherlands, and Portugal. On 5 August 1969 Capt. William F. Chaires assumed command, and on 2 September *Yorktown* departed Norfolk for what became her last deployment. Her new air group, CVSG-56, included two S-2E Tracker squadrons, VS-24 and VS-27; HS-3 with SH-3D Sea King helicopters; and two detachments—VAW-121 Det. 10 with the E-1B Tracer and VSF-1 Det. 10 with the A-4C Skyhawk.

She participated in the major NATO exercise Operation Peacekeeper in the North Atlantic from 17 to 23 September, providing ASW and SAR support for the participating forces.

When the exercise ended *Yorktown* visited in October and November northern European ports. After each visit—Brest, France, and Rotterdam in the Netherlands—*Yorktown* put to sea for a series of hunter-killer ASW exercises. She visited Kiel, Germany, on 11 November, Germany's National Day of Mourning (the equivalent of Remembrance Day, Veterans Day, etc., elsewhere); an estimated 70,000 people jammed the streets and stood in the cold to tour the carrier. (After 5,000 visitors had boarded the ship, the local chief of police requested that the visiting be ended: police were unable to control the crowds mobbing the pier.) *Yorktown* also stopped at Copenhagen, Denmark, and at Portsmouth, England. While entering Portsmouth, a "saluting port," passing honors were exchanged with the Royal Navy shore establishments HMS *Dolphin* and HMS *Vernon*. *Yorktown*'s crew manned the rails as the British played "The Star Spangled Banner" and the *Yorktown* band played "God Save the Queen" in reply. *Yorktown* gave 21-gun and 17-gun salutes. *Yorktown* got under way for Norfolk on 1 December, arriving on the 11th, in time for holiday leave.

During the first half of 1970 *Yorktown* operated out of Norfolk and began preparations for inactivation. *Yorktown* was decommissioned on 27 June 1970 at Philadelphia, Pennsylvania. She remained berthed with the Philadelphia Group, Atlantic Reserve Fleet for almost three years. On 1 June 1973 *Yorktown* was struck from the Navy List. In 1974, the Navy Department approved the donation of *Yorktown* to the Patriots Point Development Authority, Charleston, South Carolina. She was towed from Bayonne, New Jersey, to Charleston in June 1975 and was formally dedicated as a memorial on the 200th anniversary of the Navy, 13 October 1975.

A VS-27 S-2E preparing to launch. (U.S. Navy)

E-1B from VAW-121 Det 10, 1969. (U.S. Navy)

A VSF-1 Det 10 A-4B during *Yorktown*'s 1969 European deployment. (U.S. Navy)

Refueling at sea during *Yorktown*'s 1969 European deployment. (U.S. Navy)

Yorktown at Patriots Point Naval & Maritime Museum. (Patriots Point)

PATRIOTS POINT

The Patriots Point Naval & Maritime Museum in Mount Pleasant, South Carolina, is located at the mouth of the Cooper River in Charleston Harbor across from Charleston. The museum was the idea of Charles F. Hyatt, a former merchant marine and naval officer, who wanted to develop an area that had once been a dump for dredged mud into an attraction that related the history of small combatant ships of the U.S. Navy. In 1974, when the Navy Department approved the donation of *Yorktown* to the Patriots Point Development Authority, it was with the caveat that the ship be accepted in the condition in which she was. *Yorktown* arrived under tow in Charleston in June 1975 from Bayonne. After dedication, *Yorktown* was opened to the public on 3 January 1976. Since then Patriots Point has added or changed other ships and displays to become one of the largest maritime museums in the United States and has been added to the National Register of Historic Places.

The destroyer *Laffey* was added in 1978 and the submarine *Clamagore* in May 1981. (*Laffey* was under repair from 2009 to 2012, and *Clamagore* was towed away for scrapping in 2022.) The first nuclear-powered merchant ship, NS *Savannah*, was added in October 1981. (*Savannah* was moved to the James River Merchant Marine Reserve Fleet at Fort Eustis, Virginia, in 1994 after being dry-docked in Baltimore for repairs.)

Replica of Vietnam War riverine base, Patriots Point. (Patriots Point)

In 1984 the Coast Guard cutter USCGC *Comanche* was acquired but was not opened to the public. It was replaced by the cutter USCGC *Ingham* that same year. (*Comanche*, damaged by Hurricane Hugo in 1989, was removed from the museum in 1992 and sunk 12 miles offshore from Charleston as an artificial fishing reef. *Ingham* was removed by the Coast Guard in 2009 and towed to Key West, Florida, to be part of the Key West Maritime Memorial Museum.) In 1993 a replica of a Vietnam War–era naval base was opened, and a Medal of Honor museum, with biographies of all medal recipients, is now part of the exhibits.

An extensive collection of historic aircraft is also on display on board *Yorktown*, as well as artifacts from the Apollo 8 space mission.

The "boilerplate" practice Apollo 8 capsule on display on the hangar deck. (Patriots Point)

Charles F. Hyatt

Charles F. Hyatt led a life marked by civic contributions to his community, staunch patriotism, and influential leadership in the development of Patriots Point. In 1945, he attended the Merchant Marine Academy at Kings Point, New York, and from 1945 to 1950 sailed in the Atlantic and Pacific, and around the world three times. After his service as a merchant marine officer he served on active duty in the Navy during the Korean War, retiring as a lieutenant in the Naval Reserve. Earning a degree in finance and banking in 1955, he worked in the banking industry until retiring in 1991, after which he became a real estate broker. In 1973, he was appointed by South Carolina governor John West to study the feasibility of a naval museum and to make recommendations to the state legislature. He was appointed as chairman of the Patriots Point Development Authority the following year and served in that capacity for sixteen years. He was instrumental in clearing the title to the land at Patriots Point so that the state of South Carolina would always have a clear title and was appointed an Honorary Admiral of the South Carolina Navy. He was also a member of the USS *Yorktown* Association board of directors. He died at his home in 2012.

Clark Reynolds

Noted historian and author Clark G. Reynolds had a long-lasting association with naval history, particularly the development of naval aviation. He developed this interest at an early age when his uncle, F. Robert Reynolds, who had served on board *Yorktown* as an ensign from 1943 to 1944 and then as a lieutenant (junior grade), wrote letters home to his nephew. His uncle was flag aide to Rear Adm. J. J. Clark till the end of the war. After earning a bachelor of arts degree in 1961 from the University of California, Santa Barbara, a master of arts degree in 1963 from Duke University, and a PhD in 1964, he began his career as an associate professor at the Naval Academy from 1964 to 1968. From there, he went to the University of Maine, where he and another professor conducted seminars in maritime and regional history. From 1976 to 1978 he was a full professor, later holding the rank of captain in the merchant marine at the Merchant Marine Academy at Kings Point, New York. Aside from a brief stint at Mississippi State University in 1979, he spent most of his time between 1978 and 1988 as an independent scholar, working as the part-time curator and historian at Patriots Point. In this capacity he authored the application to the National Park Service in 1982 to place *Yorktown* on the National Register of Historic Places. From 1988 until his retirement in 2002 he was at the College of Charleston. He died on 10 December 2005. He won numerous awards for his contributions to naval history, and his extensive bibliography includes works that are connected with *Yorktown: The Fighting Lady: The New* Yorktown *in the Pacific War* (1986) and two works he coauthored, *Carrier Admiral* with J. J. Clark (1967) and *The Saga of Smokey Stover* (see chapter 6) with Elisha Terrill Stover (1974).

Aircraft on Display

The *Yorktown* displays aircraft from all eras either on the hangar deck or flight deck. Several helicopters are found in the Vietnam Experience nearby; the QH-50 Drone Anti-Submarine Helicopter (DASH) is on *Laffey*. The World War II–era aircraft on display on the hangar deck include a Grumman F4F Wildcat in markings from early 1942, a Douglas SBD Dauntless in *Yorktown* markings, a Grumman F6F Hellcat in tricolor camouflage with the "G-symbol" tail markings introduced in January 1945, a General Motors TBM Avenger, an FG-1D Corsair (the version built by Goodyear and flown by VBF-88 in 1945), and a Stearman N2S primary trainer suspended from the overhead. Although too late to see service in World War II the AD-4N version of the Skyraider in the markings of VA-65 is there as well. While not a Navy aircraft, a very rare B-25B version of the Mitchell bomber painted in the colors of Ted Lawson's "Ruptured Duck" (as seen in the movie *30 Seconds over Tokyo*) is also displayed.

Most of the displays are on the flight deck, however: Grumman A-6E Intruder in the markings of VA-75 on board *Independence*, a Grumman E-1B Tracer, a Douglass EA-3B "Electric Whale" version of the Skywarrior, a Grumman F-14 Tomcat in the markings of VF-154, a McDonnell Douglas F-4J Phantom II from Marine Fighter Attack Squadron (VMFA) 333, a Vought F-8K Crusader from VF-154, a Grumman S-2E Tracker from VS-23, a Lockheed S3-B Viking, a Sikorsky SH-3G Sea King from HS-4, and a McDonnell Douglas F/A-18A Hornet in the colors of the Blue Angels.

The helicopters in the Vietnam Experience include a Bell AH-1J Sea Cobra in Marine markings, a Boeing Vertol CH-46E Sea Knight from Marine Medium Helicopter Squadron (HMM) 164, a Sikorsky UH-34D Seahorse in Marine markings, and two Bell UH-1 Iroquois "Hueys"—an Army UH-1 and a Navy UH-1M.

A rare B-25B on display on the hangar deck. Another aircraft on the hangar deck is the TF-9J, the trainer version of the Cougar. (Patriots Point)

An F/A-18A Hornet in the colors of the Blue Angels. Note the awards displayed on the bridge wing. (Patriots Point)

Commanding Officers

Commissioned	**15 April 1943**
Capt. Joseph J. Clark	15 April 1943–10 February 1944
Capt. Ralph E. Jennings	10 February 1944–29 September 1944
Capt. Thomas S. Combs	29 September 1944–23 April 1945
Capt. Walter F. Boone	23 April 1945–19 November 1945
Capt. Maurice E. Browder	19 November 1945–16 July 1946
Cdr. Charles T. Fitzgerald	16 July 1946–26 December 1946
Cdr. Malcolm C. Reeves	26 December 1946–9 January 1947
Decommissioned	**9 January 1947**
Recommissioned	**20 February 1953**
Capt. William M. Nation	20 February 1953–3 August 1953
Capt. Arnold W. McKechnie	3 August 1953–5 August 1954
Capt. Gerald L. Huff	5 August 1954–15 July 1955
Capt. Emmett O'Beirne	15 July 1955–14 September 1956
Capt. Edward E. Colestock	14 September 1956–28 September 1957
Capt. James O. Cobb	28 September 1957–19 August 1958
Capt. Porter F. Bedell	19 August 1958–6 June 1959
Capt. Louis H. Bauer	6 June 1959–19 May 1960
Capt. Charles E. Gibson	19 May 1960–10 June 1961
Capt. William G. Privette Jr.	10 June 1961–14 June 1962
Capt. Waller C. Moore	14 June 1962–28 June 1963
Capt. James P. Lynch	28 June 1963–22 June 1964
Capt. Raymond S. Osterhoudt	22 June 1964–11 June 1965
Capt. James B. Cain	11 June 1965–7 May 1966
Capt. William M. McCulley Jr.	7 May 1966–20 July 1967
Capt. William L. Bennett	20 July 1967–26 July 1968
Capt. John G. Fifield	26 July 1968–5 August 1969
Capt. William F. Chaires	5 August 1969–22 April 1970
Cdr. Owen A. Kidd	22 April 1970–27 June 1970
Decommissioned	**27 June 1970**

CV-10 awards as displayed on the port side of the island overlooking the flight deck. (Patriots Point)

Awards

Precedence of awards is from top to bottom, left to right.

Top Row:
Presidential Unit Citation / China Service Medal (extended)

2nd Row:
Navy Meritorious Unit Commendation / American Campaign Medal / Asiatic-Pacific Campaign Medal (11 stars)

3rd Row:
World War II Victory Medal / Navy Occupation Service Medal ("Asia" clasp) / National Defense Service Medal (2)

4th Row:
Korean Service Medal / Armed Forces Expeditionary Medal (4) / Vietnam Service Medal (4 stars)

5th Row:
Philippine Presidential Unit Citation / Republic of Vietnam Meritorious Unit Citation (Gallantry Cross Medal with Palm) / Philippine Liberation Medal

6th Row:
United Nations Korean Medal / Republic of Vietnam Campaign Medal / Republic of Korea War Service Medal (retroactive)

Laffey

USS *Laffey* (DD-724) was an *Allen M. Sumner*–class destroyer named for the *Benson*-class destroyer *Laffey* (DD-459), lost in action on 13 November 1942 during the Naval Battle of Guadalcanal. Commissioned in 1944 the new *Laffey* served in the Atlantic and participated in the D-Day landings in June before heading for the Pacific. On 16 April 1945, on a radar picket station north of Okinawa, she was attacked by numerous kamikazes. *Laffey* survived despite being badly damaged by four bombs, six kamikaze crashes, and strafing that killed 32 and wounded 71. She was not repaired before the end of the war but would go on to serve in the Korean War. She returned to the Atlantic and served until 1975, the last of her class to be decommissioned. She became a museum ship at Patriots Point. When leaks in her hull were discovered in 2008, officials obtained a loan from the state to have her towed to a dry-dock where her hull was repaired with thicker plating, extensive welding, and new paint. When she returned to Patriots Point on 25 January 2012 more than a dozen former crew members were among the crowd on hand to welcome her. As one veteran said, "This means a lot of years of fighting to get her saved again. The Germans tried to sink her. The Japanese tried to sink her and then she tried to sink herself sitting here. She's whipped them all and she's back again."

FROM THE PATRIOTS POINT NAVAL & MARITIME MUSEUM

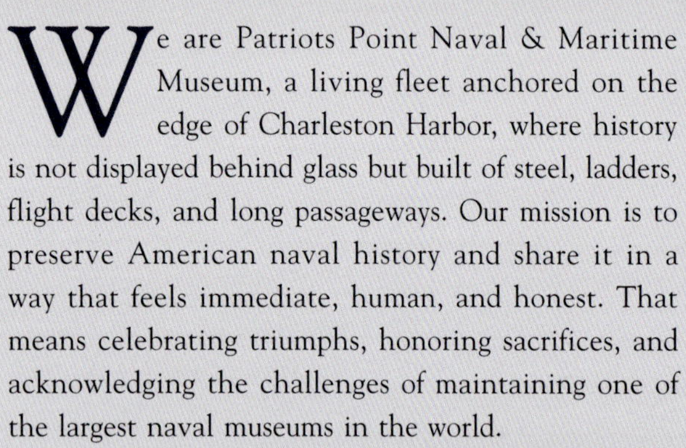

We are Patriots Point Naval & Maritime Museum, a living fleet anchored on the edge of Charleston Harbor, where history is not displayed behind glass but built of steel, ladders, flight decks, and long passageways. Our mission is to preserve American naval history and share it in a way that feels immediate, human, and honest. That means celebrating triumphs, honoring sacrifices, and acknowledging the challenges of maintaining one of the largest naval museums in the world.

At the heart of everything we do stands USS *Yorktown* (CV 10), the legendary World War II aircraft carrier known as the "Fighting Lady." Commissioned in April 1943 after a remarkably fast construction period, *Yorktown* entered service at a moment when the outcome of the Pacific War was still far from certain. Over the course of the conflict, she earned 11 battle stars, carried thousands of sailors and aviators into combat, and became a floating city dedicated entirely

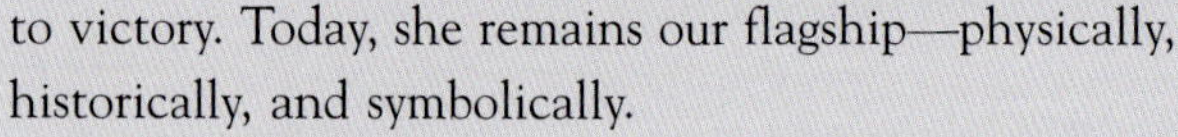

to victory. Today, she remains our flagship—physically, historically, and symbolically.

A visit to Patriots Point almost always begins aboard *Yorktown*, and for good reason. Her sheer scale tells a story before a single exhibit is read. From the flight deck overlooking Charleston Harbor, visitors can grasp the enormity of naval aviation and the coordination required to operate a carrier at war. Below decks, the ship becomes more intimate. The hangar bay, now home to aircraft and immersive exhibits, gives insight into daily life aboard ship—how sailors slept, ate, worked, and waited. As guests descend further into engineering spaces, medical areas, and command centers, *Yorktown* reveals herself not just as a weapon of war, but as a place where real people lived under extraordinary pressure.

Yorktown's story does not end with World War II. After being modernized for the jet age, she later played a quieter but no less historic role in the space race. In December 1968, she served as the recovery ship for Apollo 8, welcoming astronauts back to Earth after humanity's first voyage to the Moon. That moment connects the ship not only to naval history, but to one of the most profound achievements in human exploration—an intersection of sea power, technology, and national ambition.

Surrounding *Yorktown* is our aircraft collection, displayed on her flight deck and within the hangar bay. These aircraft span multiple generations, from propeller-driven World War II designs to Cold War–era jets, illustrating the rapid evolution of naval aviation. Walking among them reinforces the reality that aircraft carriers exist to support aviation, and that every plane represents crews, risks, and missions that once depended on the ship beneath their wheels.

Moored alongside our carrier is USS *Laffey* (DD 724), a World War II destroyer known as "The Ship That Would Not Die." In contrast to *Yorktown*'s vast spaces, *Laffey* offers a tighter, more intense experience. Her narrow passageways and compact combat stations reflect the speed, vulnerability, and resilience of destroyer crews who escorted carriers, hunted submarines, and endured relentless attacks. Together, *Yorktown* and *Laffey* tell complementary stories of naval warfare—one massive and complex, the other fast, exposed, and unyielding.

Beyond our ships, Patriots Point expands into immersive and interpretive spaces that explore later chapters of American military history. The Vietnam Experience is a 2.5-acre outdoor exhibit designed to place visitors inside a Vietnam-era naval and Marine Corps environment. With helicopters, patrol boats, vehicles, and recreated base areas, it emphasizes context and perspective, allowing visitors to better understand the landscape, technology, and complexity of that conflict.

Preservation itself is a constant, demanding effort. Salt air, humidity, corrosion, environmental regulations, and the sheer size of our vessels require ongoing maintenance and long-term planning. Projects such as fuel removal, structural repairs, and environmental remediation are essential to keeping these ships safe, stable, and open to the public. Every admission ticket, program, event, and membership directly supports that work.

Patriots Point is not a static memorial—it is an active commitment. We preserve these ships not just to remember the past, but to ensure future generations can stand where history happened, feel its scale, and understand what it took to build, operate, and sustain American sea power. When you walk our decks, you are not just visiting a museum. You are stepping aboard history—and helping keep it afloat.

World of Warships is a free-to-play, naval warfare–themed massively multiplayer online game developed and published by Wargaming. Like *World of Tanks* and *World of Warplanes*, it allows players to command historic vehicles in player-versus-player battles, cooperative matches against bots, or advanced player-versus-environment (PvE) modes. *World of Warships* launched on PC in 2015, followed by console releases under the title *World of Warships: Legends* for PlayStation®4 and Xbox One in 2019, and for PlayStation®5 and Xbox Series X/S in April 2021.

Developed by Lesta Studios in St. Petersburg, Russia, *World of Warships* (PC) has more than 44 million registered players across five global servers. Over 500 dedicated staff members work on a four-week update cycle, regularly introducing new features, ships, and mechanics to keep gameplay fresh and welcoming for new players. The game includes more than 400 ships across 12 in-game nations. Each ship is designed using historical documents and original blueprints from the first half of the 20th century, with development taking an average of two to six man-months per vessel.

Players can choose from more than 20 ports, 10 of which are recreated from historical harbors and port towns. There are four primary ship classes—destroyers, cruisers, battleships, and aircraft carriers—each offering a distinct gameplay experience. Submarines have been in testing cycles since 2018 and, following extensive changes based on player feedback, are expected to launch as a fifth class in the near future. Ships are organized into tiers ranging from I to X, with tier X representing the pinnacle of naval engineering from World War II and the early Cold War era. Each warship is led by a naval commander, with many commanders available, including more than 10 iconic historical figures. Battles take place across more than 40 maps, with seven permanent or seasonal Battle Types: Co-op Battles, Random Battles, Ranked Battles, Clan Battles, Brawls, Scenarios, and Training. These Battle Types support four Battle Modes: Standard, Domination, Epicenter, and Arms Race.

Aircraft carriers have been part of *World of Warships* (PC) since launch and focus on squadron-based gameplay, allowing players to strike across the map, scout enemy positions, and counter opposing aircraft. Originally, carriers featured a "strategic" control system using a tactical map to assign missions to multiple squadrons simultaneously. In Update 0.8.0 (January 2019), this gameplay was completely reworked to give players direct control of a single squadron, requiring them to evade anti-aircraft fire and manually conduct attack runs. The game features U.S. aircraft carriers such as *Langley*, *Ranger*, *Lexington*, *Midway*, and *Saipan*, with additional ships planned for the future. In *World of Warships: Legends*, aircraft carriers are currently available for the U.S., Japan, and Germany, with the American branch including *Langley*, *Ranger*, and *Lexington*.

Developed by the same team as the PC version, *World of Warships: Legends* is a standalone experience designed to take full advantage of home console capabilities. It brings large-scale online naval combat to consoles for the first time, alongside exclusive content and features tailored to the platform. The game is available on the PlayStation® Store and Microsoft Store, offering battles across diverse maps and warships, with HDR support on PlayStation®4 and Xbox One X, full 4K support on PlayStation®4 Pro, PlayStation®5, and Xbox One X, and enhanced visuals across all platforms.

Wargaming also preserves naval history through a documentary series focused on museum ships. Since 2014, more than 50 episodes have been released, covering famous vessels from countries including the United States, Great Britain, Canada, France, Japan, Germany, Greece, Australia, Sweden, Poland, the Russian Federation, and China. These documentaries explore all major warship classes involved in the world